S0-CBA-834

Better Homes and Gardens®

Hometown
FAVORITES

Delicious, down-home recipes

Volume 4

Meredith Consumer Marketing
Des Moines, Iowa

Better Homes and Gardens
Hometown Favorites

MEREDITH CONSUMER MARKETING
Vice President, Consumer Marketing: Janet Donnelly
Consumer Product Marketing Director: Steve Swanson
Consumer Product Marketing Manager: Wendy Merical
Business Director: Ron Clingman
Senior Production Manager: George Susral

WATERBURY PUBLICATIONS, INC.
Editorial Director: Lisa Kingsley
Associate Editor: Tricia Bergman
Creative Director: Ken Carlson
Associate Design Director: Doug Samuelson
Contributing Art Director: Mindy Samuelson
Contributing Copy Editors: Terri Fredrickson, Peg Smith
Contributing Indexer: Elizabeth T. Parson

BETTER HOMES AND GARDENS MAGAZINE
Editor in Chief: Gayle Goodson Butler
Art Director: Michael D. Belknap
Deputy Editor, Food and Entertaining: Nancy Wall Hopkins
Senior Food Editor: Richard Swearinger
Associate Food Editor: Erin Simpson
Editorial Assistant: Renee Irey

MEREDITH NATIONAL MEDIA GROUP
President: Tom Harty
Vice President, Production: Bruce Heston

MEREDITH CORPORATION
Chairman and Chief Executive Officer: Stephen M. Lacy

In Memoriam: E.T. Meredith III (1933–2003)

Copyright© 2012 by Meredith Corporation.
Des Moines, Iowa.
First Edition. All rights reserved.
Printed in China.
ISSN: 1944-6349 ISBN: 978-0-696-30098-1

Better Homes and Gardens

Test Kitchen

Our seal assures you that every recipe in *Hometown Favorites* has been tested in the Better Homes and Gardens Test Kitchen. This means that each recipe is practical and reliable, and meets our high standards of taste appeal. We guarantee your satisfaction with this book for as long as you own it.

All of us at Meredith Consumer Marketing are dedicated to providing you with information and ideas to enhance your home. We welcome your comments and suggestions. Write to us at: Meredith Consumer Marketing, 1716 Locust St., Des Moines, IA 50309-3023.

Pictured on front cover:
Peach Turnovers, page 184

Contents

CHAPTER 1

Appetizers

These tasty bites are all dressed up and ready to make a grand appearance at munch and mingle gatherings. Not planning a party? Once you check out these delicious bites, you just might change your mind!

8

22

25

White Chocolate Snack Mix

Watch fiber-rich shredded wheat cereal squares go absolutely yummy in this sensational make-ahead mix.

1. Line an extra-large baking sheet with waxed paper or parchment paper; set aside. In an extra-large bowl gently combine cereal, graham crackers, pretzels, rice cakes, marshmallows, raisins, and nuts.

2. In a medium saucepan combine white chocolate, cream, and corn syrup. Cook and stir over low heat until nearly melted; remove from heat and stir gently until smooth. Stir in almond extract.

3. Pour warm chocolate mixture over cereal mixture; toss gently to coat. Immediately spread mixture onto the prepared baking sheet. Cool until chocolate is set (up to 12 hours). Break into pieces.

FOR 56 SERVINGS: Prepare using method above, except in Step 1 line two extra-large baking sheets with waxed paper or parchment paper. In Step 3 spread mixture onto both of the prepared baking sheets.

PER ¼-CUP SERVING *105 cal., 5 g total fat (2 g sat. fat), 4 mg chol., 75 mg sodium, 14 g carbo., 1 g fiber, 2 g pro.*

START TO FINISH: **45 MINUTES**

28 servings	ingredients	56 servings
1 cup	bite-size wheat or rice square cereal, bite-size shredded wheat biscuits	2 cups
1 cup	broken graham crackers, graham crackers with cinnamon-sugar topping, or chocolate-covered graham crackers	2 cups
1 cup	pretzel sticks	2 cups
1 cup	broken rice cakes	2 cups
½ cup	tiny marshmallows	1 cup
½ cup	raisins or mixed dried fruit bits	1 cup
½ cup	whole or slivered almonds or cashews	1 cup
8 oz.	white baking chocolate, chopped	1 lb.
3 Tbsp.	whipping cream	⅓ cup
2 tsp.	light-color corn syrup	1 Tbsp.
¼ tsp.	almond extract	½ tsp.

Ricotta Dip for Fruit

To make this creamy dip even more healthful, purchase low-fat, part-skim ricotta. If you're lucky enough to have leftovers, put a thick smear of the dip on a ham or chicken sandwich topped with thin apple or pear slices.

1. For dip, in a blender or food processor combine ricotta cheese, cream cheese, orange juice, and powdered sugar. Cover and blend or process until smooth. In a medium bowl stir together cheese mixture and yogurt. If desired, cover and chill dip up to 24 hours.

2. Serve with assorted fresh fruit.

FOR 24 SERVINGS: Prepare using method above, except in Step 1 process ingredients in two batches.

PER 2-TABLESPOON SERVING *94 cal., 4 g total fat (3 g sat. fat), 14 mg chol., 72 mg sodium, 12 g carbo., 1 g fiber, 3 g pro.*

*NOTE: For a richer, creamier dip, substitute whole milk ricotta cheese for low-fat ricotta cheese.

PREP: 15 MINUTES
CHILL: 24 HOURS

12 servings	ingredients	24 servings
½ cup	low-fat ricotta cheese*	1 cup
4 oz.	cream cheese, softened	1 8-oz. pkg.
3 Tbsp.	orange juice	6 Tbsp.
2 Tbsp.	powdered sugar	¼ cup
1 6-oz. container	vanilla low-fat yogurt	2 6-oz. containers
6 cups	cubed cantaloupe, cubed honeydew melon, pineapple chunks, and/or strawberries	12 cups

Very Veggie Dip

More than a dip, this veggie-packed appetizer is a great spread to keep on hand for spreading on after-school wrap sandwich snacks.

1. In a medium mixing bowl beat sour cream, cream cheese, and milk with an electric mixer on low to medium until smooth. Stir in sweet pepper, zucchini, carrot, and chives. Stir in salt and pepper.

2. To serve, stir dip. Serve with vegetables, crackers, and/or tortilla chips.

FOR 32 SERVINGS: Prepare using method above, except in Step 1 mix ingredients in a large bowl.

PER SERVING 39 cal., 3 g total fat (2 g sat. fat), 10 mg chol., 76 mg sodium, 2 g carbo., 0 g fiber, 1 g pro.

SOUTH-OF-THE-BORDER VEGGIE DIP: Prepare as directed, except omit the sweet pepper, zucchini, carrot, and chives. Stir in ⅔ cup purchased salsa. For 32 servings, stir in 1⅓ cups purchased salsa.

START TO FINISH: **20 MINUTES**

16 servings	ingredients	32 servings
1 8-oz. carton	light sour cream	2 8-oz. cartons
½ of an 8-oz. pkg.	reduced-fat cream cheese (Neufchâtel)	1 8-oz. pkg.
1 Tbsp.	fat-free milk	2 Tbsp.
¼ cup	finely chopped red or yellow sweet pepper	½ cup
¼ cup	finely chopped zucchini	½ cup
2 Tbsp.	shredded carrot	¼ cup
1 Tbsp.	snipped fresh chives	2 Tbsp.
¼ tsp.	salt	½ tsp.
¼ tsp.	black pepper	½ tsp.
	Fresh cut-up vegetables, whole grain crackers, and/or multigrain tortilla chips	

Club Sandwich Dip

Cubed garlic bread makes a dynamite dunker for this creamy dip.

1. In a 3½- or 4-quart slow cooker, combine turkey, ham, process cheese, cream cheese, mayonnaise, and mustard.

2. Cover and cook on high-heat setting for 1 to 2 hours or until cheeses are melted, stirring after 1 hour.

3. Serve immediately or keep warm, covered, on warm setting or low-heat setting for up to 2 hours, stirring occasionally. Before serving, stir in half of the bacon. Top with the remaining bacon, tomatoes, and green onion. Serve with toast points and/or vegetables.

FOR 40 SERVINGS: Prepare using method above, except use a 5- to 6-quart slow cooker in Step 1.

PER ¼-CUP SERVING 177 cal., 13 g total fat (6 g sat. fat), 46 mg chol., 578 mg sodium, 3 g carbo., 0 g fiber, 11 g pro.

PREP: 20 MINUTES
COOK: 1 HOUR (HIGH)

20 servings	ingredients	40 servings
1 lb.	smoked turkey, chopped	2 lb.
8 oz.	cooked ham, chopped	1 lb.
8 oz.	process Swiss or American cheese, torn	1 lb.
1 8-oz. pkg.	cream cheese, cut up	2 8-oz. pkgs.
1 cup	light mayonnaise	2 cups
2 tsp.	Dijon mustard	4 tsp.
6 slices	bacon, crisp-cooked, drained, and crumbled	12 slices
½ cup	cherry or grape tomatoes, coarsely chopped	1 cup
1 Tbsp.	sliced green onion	2 Tbsp.
	Whole wheat toast points and/or assorted cut-up vegetables	

Cheesy Shrimp Dip

No need to buy premium shrimp for this delightful dip—any variety on sale will do just fine. The little crustaceans are most likely to be on sale between Thanksgiving and Christmas, so it's a good idea to stock up then.

15 servings	ingredients	30 servings
2 8-oz. pkgs.	cream cheese, cubed	4 8 oz. pkgs.
2 cups	shredded fontina cheese	4 cups
½ cup	finely shredded Parmesan cheese	1 cup
1 cup	half-and-half or light cream	2 cups
½ cup	sliced green onions	1 cup
2 Tbsp.	dry white wine	¼ cup
2 Tbsp.	Dijon mustard	¼ cup
¼ tsp.	cayenne pepper	½ tsp.
1 lb.	fresh or frozen peeled and deveined cooked shrimp	2 lb.
2 tsp.	finely shredded lemon peel	¼ tsp.
	Assorted cut-up vegetables	
	Chopped green onion	

1. In a 3½- or 4-quart slow cooker stir together cream cheese, fontina cheese, and Parmesan cheese. Stir in half-and-half, green onions, wine, mustard, and cayenne pepper.

2. Cover and cook on low-heat setting for 3 hours or on high-heat setting for 1½ hours.

3. Thaw shrimp, if frozen. Chop shrimp; stir shrimp and lemon peel into cheese mixture.

4. Serve immediately or keep warm, covered, on warm setting or low-heat setting for up to 2 hours. Serve with vegetables. If desired, garnish with green onion.

FOR 30 SERVINGS: Prepare using method above, except use a 5- to 6-quart slow cooker.

PER ¼-CUP SERVING *283 cal., 20 g total fat (12 g sat. fat), 124 mg chol., 625 mg sodium, 3 g carbo., 0 g fiber, 18 g pro.*

Italian Grinder Dip

This dip is so good you could eat it with a spoon—but if you have to mind your manners, spoon it over chewy ciabatta bread strips.

1. In a large skillet cook ground beef, sausage, onion, and garlic over medium-high heat until meat is brown, using a wooden spoon to break up meat as it cooks. Drain off fat.

2. In a 3½- or 4-quart slow cooker combine meat mixture, sweet pepper, mushrooms, fennel seeds, oregano, basil, and crushed red pepper. Stir in pizza sauce.

3. Cover and cook on low-heat setting for 4 to 5 hours or on high-heat setting for 2 to 2½ hours. Serve on toasted bread and sprinkle with cheese.

FOR 44 SERVINGS: Prepare using method above, except in Step 1 use a very large skillet. In Step 2 use a 5- or 6-quart slow cooker.

PER 3-TABLESPOON SERVING *148 cal., 12 g total fat (4 g sat. fat), 32 mg chol., 217 mg sodium, 3 g carbo., 1 g fiber, 7 g pro.*

PREP: 25 MINUTES
COOK: 4 HOURS (LOW) OR 2 HOURS (HIGH)

22 servings	ingredients	44 servings
1 lb.	ground beef	2 lb.
1 lb.	bulk Italian sausage	2 lb.
1 cup	chopped onion	2 cups
3 cloves	garlic, minced	6 cloves
¾ cup	chopped green sweet pepper	1½ cups
1 4-oz. can (drained weight)	sliced mushrooms, drained	2 4-oz. cans (drained weight)
1 tsp.	fennel seeds, crushed	2 tsp.
1 tsp.	dried oregano, crushed	2 tsp.
1 tsp.	dried basil, crushed	2 tsp.
½ tsp.	crushed red pepper	1 tsp.
1 15-oz. can	pizza sauce	2 15-oz. cans
	Sliced garlic bread and/or ciabatta bread, toasted	
	Shredded mozzarella cheese	

Spinach and Roasted Red Pepper Dip

Sometimes you have to give into cravings. When you just need a really great snack, skip the crackers and flatbread and head straight to crispy tortilla chips for dunking into this hot cheesy dip.

1. Preheat oven to 350°F. In a large bowl stir together mozzarella cheese, yogurt, mayonnaise, 2 tablespoons of the Parmesan cheese, flour, and mustard. Stir in spinach, roasted red peppers, and 2 tablespoons of the green onions. Spread mixture evenly into an ungreased 1-quart ovenproof shallow dish. Sprinkle with the remaining 2 tablespoons Parmesan cheese.

2. Bake, uncovered, for 15 to 20 minutes or until edges are bubbly and mixture is heated through. Sprinkle with the remaining 2 tablespoons green onions. Serve with sweet pepper strips, and crackers or flatbread.

FOR 72 SERVINGS: Prepare using method above, except in Step 1 spread mixture into an ungreased 2-quart ovenproof shallow dish. Sprinkle remaining ¼ cup Parmesan cheese.

PER 2-TABLESPOON SERVING *21 cal., 2 g total fat (0 g sat. fat), 3 mg chol., 47 mg sodium, 1 g carbo., 1 g pro.*

PREP: **20 MINUTES**
BAKE: **15 MINUTES**
OVEN: **350°F**

36 servings	ingredients	72 servings
½ cup	shredded part-skim mozzarella cheese	1 cup
½ cup	plain low-fat yogurt	1 cup
½ cup	mayonnaise	1 cup
¼ cup	grated Parmesan cheese	½ cup
1 Tbsp.	all-purpose flour	2 Tbsp.
1 tsp.	Dijon mustard	2 tsp.
1 cup	loosely packed fresh spinach leaves, coarsely chopped	2 cups
¾ cup	bottled roasted red sweet peppers, drained and chopped	1½ cups
¼ cup	thinly sliced green onions	½ cup
3	red and/or yellow sweet peppers, seeded and cut into strips	6
	Assorted crackers or flatbread	

Marinated Feta and Olives

Grab plenty of wooden picks for this fan-favorite appetizer. The mixture may be marinated for hours, but it will be devoured in minutes, so you might want to make a double batch.

1. In a large glass or stainless-steel bowl combine cheese cubes, Kalamata olives, green olives, sweet peppers, and onion wedges.

2. In a screw-top jar combine olive oil, vinegar, garlic, thyme, oregano, and pepper. Cover and shake well. Pour over mixture in bowl; toss gently to coat.

3. Cover and marinate in the refrigerator for 4 to 6 hours before serving. Serve with picks.

PER SERVING 138 cal., 12 g total fat (4 g sat. fat), 20 mg chol., 444 mg sodium, 4 g carbo., 1 g fiber, 3 g pro.

PREP: **30 MINUTES**
MARINATE: **4 HOURS**

20 servings	ingredients	40 servings
1 lb.	feta cheese, cut into ½-inch cubes	2 lb.
1 cup	pitted Kalamata olives	2 cups
1 cup	pitted green olives	2 cups
½ cup	bottled roasted red sweet peppers, cut into strips	1 cup
1	red onion, cut into thin wedges	2
½ cup	olive oil	1 cup
½ cup	balsamic vinegar	1 cup
4 cloves	garlic, minced	8 cloves
1 Tbsp.	snipped fresh thyme leaves	2 Tbsp.
2 tsp.	snipped fresh oregano	4 tsp.
½ tsp.	cracked black pepper	1 tsp.

Ripe Olive Cheese Balls

If you're pressed for time, feel free to skip the labor-intensive ball rolling in favor of just whipping up the ingredients and mounding the mixture in a pretty wooden bowl.

1. Place cream cheese, butter, and blue cheese in a large mixing bowl; let stand for 30 minutes to reach room temperature. Beat with an electric mixer on low until smooth. Stir in olives and green onion. Cover and chill for at least 4 hours or up to 24 hours.

2. Shape mixture loosely into one ball; cover and chill until serving time. Serve cheese ball with assorted crackers, flat bread, pita wedges, dried fruits, and/or walnut halves.

FOR 46 SERVINGS: Prepare using method above, except in Step 2 shape mixture into two balls.

MAKE-AHEAD DIRECTIONS: Prepare as directed. Place in a freezer container. Cover and freeze up to 3 months. Thaw in refrigerator overnight before serving.

PER SERVING *55 cal., 6 g total fat (3 g sat. fat), 14 mg chol., 69 mg sodium, 1 g carbo., 0 g fiber, 1 g pro.*

PREP: **15 MINUTES**
STAND: **30 MINUTES**
CHILL: **4 HOURS**

23 servings	ingredients	46 servings
1 8-oz. pkg.	cream cheese	2 8-oz. pkgs.
¼ cup	butter	½ cup
¼ cup	crumbled blue cheese	½ cup
½ 4.5-oz. can	sliced pitted ripe olives, drained	1 4.5-oz. can
1 Tbsp.	chopped green onion or snipped fresh chives	2 Tbsp.
	Assorted crackers, flat bread, toasted pita wedges, dried dates and/or dried apricots, and walnut halves	

Bacon-Pecan Tassies

As fans of sugar-glazed ham, salted caramel, and chocolate-covered potato chips know, salty mixed with sweet is an absolutely irresistible flavor combo.

1. Preheat oven to 325°F. In a medium bowl combine ½ cup butter and cream cheese. Beat with an electric mixer on medium until smooth. Stir in flour. Divide dough into 24 pieces; shape into balls. Press balls onto the bottoms and up the sides of 24 ungreased 1¾-inch muffin cups. Set aside.

2. For filling, in a medium bowl beat egg, brown sugar, and melted butter until combined. Stir in pecans and bacon. Spoon about 1 heaping teaspoon of the filling into each pastry-lined muffin cup.

3. Bake for 25 to 30 minutes or until pastry is golden brown and filling is puffed. Cool slightly in pan. Carefully transfer tassies to a wire rack; cool. If desired, sprinkle with chives.

FOR 48 SERVINGS: Prepare using method above, except in Step 1 combine 1 cup butter and cream cheese in a large bowl. Divide dough into 48 pieces; shape into balls. Press balls onto the bottoms and up the sides of 48 ungreased 1¾-inch muffin cups.

PER TASSIE *118 cal., 8 g total fat (4 g sat. fat), 25 mg chol., 62 mg sodium, 11 g carbo., 0 g fiber, 2 g pro.*

PREP: **30 MINUTES**
BAKE: **25 MINUTES**
OVEN: **325°F**

24 servings	ingredients	48 servings
½ cup	butter, softened	1 cup
1 3-oz. pkg.	cream cheese, softened	2 3-oz. pkgs.
1 cup	all-purpose flour	2 cups
1	egg	2
¾ cup	packed brown sugar	1½ cups
1 Tbsp.	butter, melted	2 Tbsp.
½ cup	coarsely chopped pecans	1 cup
2 slices	bacon, crisp-cooked, drained, and crumbled	4 slices
	Snipped fresh chives (optional)	

Flamin' Cajun Riblets

Have plenty of napkins on hand for guests who go for these spicy, finger-licking pork ribs.

PREP: 20 MINUTES
COOK: 5 HOURS (LOW) OR 2½ HOURS (HIGH)

12 servings	ingredients	24 servings
3 lb.	pork loin back ribs	6 lb.
1 Tbsp.	Cajun seasoning	2 Tbsp.
1 cup	bottled chili sauce	2 cups
½ cup	finely chopped onion	1 cup
1	serrano pepper, seeded and finely chopped*	2
2 Tbsp.	quick-cooking tapioca, crushed	¼ cup
1 tsp.	finely shredded lemon peel	2 tsp.
1 Tbsp.	lemon juice	2 Tbsp.
1 tsp.	bottled hot pepper sauce	2 tsp.
	Snipped fresh parsley (optional)	

1. Sprinkle ribs with Cajun seasoning; rub in with your fingers. Cut ribs into 4 to 5 rib portions. Place ribs in a 3½- or 4-quart slow cooker.

2. In a medium bowl combine chili sauce, onion, serrano pepper, tapioca, lemon peel, lemon juice, and hot pepper sauce. Pour sauce over ribs.

3. Cover and cook on low-heat setting for 5 to 6 hours or on high-heat setting for 2½ to 3 hours. Cut ribs into single rib portions. Serve immediately or keep covered on warm or low-heat setting up to 2 hours. (Remove any bones without meat.) If desired, sprinkle with parsley.

FOR 24 SERVINGS: Prepare using method above, except in Step 1 place ribs in a 5- to 6-quart slow cooker.

PER SERVING 231 cal., 17 g total fat (6 g sat. fat), 57 mg chol., 369 mg sodium, 7 g carbo., 1 g fiber, 12 g pro.

*TIP: Because hot chile peppers contain volatile oils that can burn your skin and eyes, avoid direct contact with chiles as much as possible. When working with chile peppers, wear plastic or rubber gloves. If your bare hands do touch the chile peppers, wash your hands and nails well with soap and water.

Saucy Apricot 'n' Spiced Meatballs

Meatballs are always the first to disappear from an appetizer buffet. To up the ante, consider serving these succulent orbs alongside a bowl of freshly cut pineapple.

1. Preheat oven to 350°F. Line a 15×10×1-inch baking pan with foil; lightly grease foil; set aside. In a medium bowl combine bread crumbs and milk. Let stand for 5 minutes. Stir in egg white, onion, dried apricots, salt, garlic, and chili powder. Add ground pork and turkey; mix well.

2. Shape mixture into 24 meatballs. Place meatballs in the prepared baking pan. Bake, uncovered, for 15 to 20 minutes or until meatballs are cooked through (160°F), checking with an instant-read thermometer. Drain off fat.

3. For the spiced apricot sauce, in a small saucepan combine apricot nectar, cornstarch, chili powder, salt, and nutmeg. Cook and stir over medium heat until thickened and bubbly. Cook and stir for 1 minute more.

4. Place meatballs in a 1½-quart slow cooker. Add spiced apricot sauce; toss gently to coat. Serve meatballs with short skewers or toothpicks. If desired, keep warm in a slow cooker on warm or low-heat setting up to 2 hours.

FOR 48 SERVINGS: Prepare using method above, except in Step 1 line two 15×10×1-inch baking pans with foil. In Step 2 shape mixture into 48 meatballs. In Step 4 place meatballs in a 3½- or 4-quart slow cooker.

PER MEATBALL 38 cal., 2 g total fat (1 g sat. fat), 8 mg chol., 78 mg sodium, 3 g carbo., 0 g fiber, 3 g pro.

PREP: 25 MINUTES
BAKE: 15 MINUTES
OVEN: 350°F

24 servings	ingredients	48 servings
½ cup	soft bread crumbs	1 cup
2 Tbsp.	fat-free milk	¼ cup
1	egg white	2
¼ cup	finely chopped onion	½ cup
¼ cup	finely snipped dried apricots	½ cup
½ tsp.	salt	1 tsp.
1 clove	garlic, minced	2 cloves
¼ tsp.	ancho chile powder or chili powder	½ tsp.
6 oz.	lean ground pork	12 oz.
6 oz.	ground raw turkey breast	12 oz.
½ cup	apricot nectar	1 cup
1 tsp.	cornstarch	2 tsp.
¼ tsp.	chili powder	½ tsp.
⅛ tsp.	salt	¼ tsp.
⅛ tsp.	ground nutmeg	¼ tsp.

Creole Turkey Meatballs

When purchasing ground turkey for these meatballs, be sure to get a package labeled "ground turkey" and not "ground turkey breast." Ground breast is simply too lean to hold together.

PREP: 25 MINUTES
BAKE: 25 MINUTES
OVEN: 375°F

30 servings	ingredients	60 servings
1	egg, lightly beaten	2
½ cup	finely chopped sweet green pepper	1 cup
½ cup	quick-cooking rolled oats	1 cup
½ cup	chopped onion	1 cup
2 Tbsp.	milk	¼ cup
1 tsp.	dried Italian seasoning, crushed	2 tsp.
1 tsp.	salt-free garlic and herb seasoning blend	2 tsp.
1 tsp.	Creole seasoning	2 tsp.
2 cloves	garlic, minced	4 cloves
1 lb.	ground raw turkey or chicken	2 lb.

1. Preheat oven to 375°F. Lightly grease a 15×10×1-inch pan; set aside. In a large bowl combine egg, sweet pepper, oats, onion, milk, Italian seasoning, salt-free seasoning, Creole seasoning, and garlic. Add turkey; mix well.

2. Shape mixture into 30 meatballs. Place meatballs in a single layer in the prepared baking pan.

3. Bake, uncovered, about 25 minutes or until cooked through (165°F), checking with an instant-read thermometer.

4. Serve meatballs with short skewers or toothpicks. If desired, keep warm in a slow cooker on warm or low-heat setting for up to 2 hours.

FOR 60 SERVINGS: Prepare using method above, except in Step 1 lightly grease two 15×10×1-inch pans. In Step 2 shape mixture into 60 meatballs.

PER MEATBALL 33 cal., 2 g total fat (0 g sat. fat), 19 mg chol., 37 mg sodium, 2 g carbo., 0 g fiber, 3 g pro.

Cranberry-Sauced Sausages

Your slow cooker is salvation with an electric cord, especially during the holidays when it will cook this Christmas classic to perfection.

1. In a large saucepan combine cranberry sauce, ketchup, lemon juice, dry mustard, and allspice. Stir in sausage links. Cook over medium-high heat until heated through, stirring occasionally.

2. Serve immediately or keep warm, covered, in a 1½- or 2-quart slow cooker on warm setting or low-heat setting for up to 2 hours.

FOR 32 SERVINGS: Prepare using method above, except use a very large saucepan in Step 1. Use a 3- or 3½-quart slow cooker in Step 2.

PER SERVING 134 cal., 7 g total fat (3 g sat. fat), 20 mg chol., 393 mg sodium, 13 g carbo., 1 g fiber, 4 g pro.

PREP: 10 MINUTES
COOK: 10 MINUTES

16 servings	ingredients	32 servings
1 16-oz. can	jellied cranberry sauce	2 16-oz. cans
⅔ cup	ketchup	1⅓ cups
2 Tbsp.	lemon juice	¼ cup
1 tsp.	dry mustard	2 tsp.
¼ tsp.	ground allspice	½ tsp.
1 16-oz. pkg.	small cooked smoked sausage links	2 16-oz. pkgs.

Italian Pepperoni-Cheese Puffs

Guests won't get enough of this fun appetizer. The perfect starter for a casual gathering or as a delicious snack for family movie night, these little pizza puffs are guaranteed to be the crowd pleaser.

PREP: 30 MINUTES
BAKE: 15 MINUTES PER BATCH
OVEN: 450°F

20 servings	ingredients	40 servings
⅔ cup	water	1⅓ cups
2 Tbsp.	shortening	4 Tbsp.
¾ cup	all-purpose flour	1½ cups
2	eggs	4
⅓ cup	finely chopped pepperoni	⅔ cup
⅓ cup	finely shredded Romano cheese	⅔ cup
1 Tbsp.	snipped fresh parsley	2 Tbsp.
Dash	garlic powder	⅛ tsp.
Dash	black pepper	⅛ tsp.
	Purchased pizza sauce, warmed (optional)	

1. Preheat oven to 450°F. Lightly grease one large baking sheet; set aside. In a large saucepan combine the water and shortening. Bring to boiling. Add flour all at once, stirring vigorously. Cook and stir until mixture forms a ball. Remove from heat. Cool for 10 minutes. Add eggs, one at a time, beating well with a wooden spoon after each addition. Stir in pepperoni, cheese, parsley, garlic powder, and pepper.

2. Drop dough by rounded teaspoons into small mounds 2 inches apart on prepared baking sheet. Bake for 15 to 17 minutes or until firm and golden brown, rotating baking sheet halfway through baking. Transfer to a wire rack. Repeat, as needed, for remaining dough. Serve warm. If desired, serve with pizza sauce.

FOR 40 SERVINGS: Prepare as above, except in Step 1 use two large baking sheets.

PER PUFF 57 cal., 4 g total fat (1 g sat. fat), 25 mg chol., 81 mg sodium, 4 g carbo., 0 g fiber, 2 g pro.

Mandarin Apricot Chicken Wings

Gingery-sweet and sticky, these Asian-style drummies are a breeze to make.

1. Preheat oven to 400°F. Arrange drummettes in a single layer in a baking pan or roasting pan lined with foil. Bake drummettes for 20 minutes.

2. Meanwhile, in a small saucepan stir together sweet-and-sour sauce, snipped apricots, hoisin sauce, soy sauce, honey, garlic, ginger, and five-spice powder. Bring to boiling; reduce heat. Simmer, uncovered, for 5 minutes. Remove from heat.

3. Brush about ¼ cup of the sauce mixture over drummettes. Sprinkle with sesame seeds. Bake about 5 minutes more or until drummettes are no longer pink in the center. Serve drummettes with remaining sauce. If desired, garnish with green onion.

FOR 16 SERVINGS: Prepare using method above, except in Step 3 brush ½ cup of the sauce over drummettes.

PER 2-DRUMETTE SERVING *129 cal., 8 g total fat (2 g sat. fat), 44 mg chol., 411 mg sodium, 11 g carbo., 0 g fiber, 8 g pro.*

PREP: 15 MINUTES
BAKE: 25 MINUTES
OVEN: 400°F

8 servings	ingredients	16 servings
16	chicken wing drummettes	32
⅔ cup	bottled sweet-and-sour sauce	1⅓ cups
½ cup	snipped dried apricots	1 cup
⅓ cup	bottled hoisin sauce	⅔ cup
¼ cup	soy sauce	½ cup
2 Tbsp.	honey	¼ cup
2 cloves	garlic, minced	4 cloves
¼ tsp.	ground ginger	½ tsp.
¼ tsp.	five-spice powder	½ tsp.
1 Tbsp.	sesame seeds, toasted	2 Tbsp.
	Green onion (optional)	

Turkey Kielbasa Bites

Simplicity is a beautiful thing. And five-ingredient recipes—like this one—are absolutely gorgeous.

PREP: **10 MINUTES**
COOK: **2½ hours (LOW)**

10 servings	ingredients	20 servings
1	orange	2
1 16-oz. pkg.	cooked turkey kielbasa, cut in 1-inch pieces	2 16-oz. pkgs.
1 14-oz. can	whole berry cranberry sauce	2 14-oz. cans
1 Tbsp.	Dijon mustard	2 Tbsp.
¼ tsp.	crushed red pepper	½ tsp.

1. Using the fine grate on a shredder, remove the zest from the orange (shred onto a sheet of waxed paper for easy clean-up). Section the orange.* Chop the orange.

2. In a 1½-quart slow cooker combine kielbasa, cranberry sauce, orange zest, chopped orange, Dijon mustard, and crushed red pepper.

3. Cover and cook on low-heat setting for 2½ to 3 hours. Serve immediately or keep warm up to 1 hour. Serve kielbasa with wooden toothpicks.

FOR 20 SERVINGS: Prepare using method above, except use a 3½- or 4-quart slow cooker.

PER SERVING *126 cal., 4 g total fat (1 g sat. fat), 28 mg chol., 441 mg sodium, 15 g carbo., 0 g fiber, 7 g pro.*

***TIP:** To section an orange, cut a thin slice from both ends of the orange. Working from the top to the bottom, cut away the peel and white part of the rind. Cut into the center of the peeled orange between one section and the membrane. Cut along the other side of the section next to the membrane to free each section. If you prefer, work over a bowl to catch the juices.

Teriyaki Chicken Rumaki

Bacon makes everything better—and you better make a lot of these, especially if you have hungry boys and men to feed.

1. Soak 4- to 6-inch wooden skewers in water for at least 30 minutes. Drain before using.

2. Preheat oven to 375°F. Cut chicken in twenty-four 1½-inch pieces. Wrap each chicken piece with 1 green onion, 1 red pepper, and a slice of bacon. Thread each skewer with wrapped chicken piece. Place in a 15×10×1-inch baking pan.

3. Bake for 8 minutes. Brush with teriyaki glaze. Bake about 16 minutes more or until bacon is cooked through.

FOR 48 SERVINGS: Prepare using method above, except cut chicken into 48 pieces in Step 2.

PER SERVING *114 cal., 9 g total fat (3 g sat. fat), 24 mg chol., 325 mg sodium, 1 g carbo., 0 g fiber, 7 g pro.*

PREP: 25 MINUTES
BAKE: 24 MINUTES
STAND: 30 MINUTES   OVEN: 375°F

24 servings	ingredients	48 servings
1 lb.	skinless, boneless chicken breast halves	2 lb.
12 slices	bacon, halved crosswise	24 slices
6	green onions, trimmed and each cut into 4 pieces	12
1 cup	narrow red sweet pepper strips	2 cups
⅓ cup	teriyaki glaze	⅔ cup

Marinated Shrimp Scampi

For easy pickup and chit-chat munchies, skewer a couple shrimp on small wooden picks with a single lemon wedge and display them in hurricane glass or clear cocktail tumblers.

PREP: 35 MINUTES
MARINATE: 1 HOUR
BROIL: 4 MINUTES

10 servings	ingredients	20 servings
2 lb.	fresh or frozen extra-jumbo shrimp in shells	4 lb.
¼ cup	olive oil	½ cup
¼ cup	dry white wine	½ cup
6 cloves	garlic, minced	12 cloves
2 tsp.	finely shredded lemon peel	4 tsp.
½ tsp.	crushed red pepper	1 tsp.
½ tsp.	salt	1 tsp.
2 Tbsp.	snipped fresh parsley	¼ cup
	Lemon wedges	

1. Thaw shrimp, if frozen. Peel and devein shrimp, leaving tails intact. Rinse shrimp and pat dry with paper towels. Place shrimp in a large resealable plastic bag set in a shallow bowl.

2. In a small bowl combine olive oil, wine, garlic, lemon peel, crushed red pepper, and salt. Pour over shrimp. Seal bag and toss gently to coat. Marinate in the refrigerator for 1 hour.

3. Remove shrimp from marinade, reserving marinade. Arrange shrimp on unheated broiler pan. Broil 4 to 5 inches from heat for 2 minutes. Turn shrimp over and brush with reserved marinade; broil 2 to 4 minutes more or until shrimp turn opaque.

4. To serve, mound shrimp on platter; sprinkle with parsley and squeeze lemon wedges over shrimp.

PER SERVING *126 cal., 4 g total fat (1 g sat. fat), 138 mg chol., 193 mg sodium, 2 g carbo., 1 g fiber, 19 g pro.*

Crab-Topped Shrimp

Shrimp doesn't always have to dress for the party in its old frock of cocktail sauce. Let it go glamorous once in a while.

1. Thaw shrimp, if frozen. Peel and devein shrimp, leaving tails intact. Rinse shrimp; pat dry with paper towels. Preheat oven to 425°F. Line a 15×10×1-inch baking pan with foil; set aside.

2. In a medium bowl beat cream cheese with an electric mixer on medium until smooth. Beat in mayonnaise, mustard, and salt. Stir in crabmeat, green onion, and roasted red pepper until combined.

3. Butterfly shrimp by cutting through the rounded side almost to the opposite side. Open shrimp and lay flat, cut side down, in prepared baking pan. Divide crab mixture among shrimp, shaping the mixture in a mound. Bring shrimp tails up and over the crab mixture.

4. Bake about 10 minutes or until shrimp are opaque. Serve warm.

FOR 32 SERVINGS: Prepare using method above, except in Step 1 line two 15×10×1-inch baking pans with foil.

PER APPETIZER *38 cal., 2 g total fat (1 g sat. fat), 23 mg chol., 90 mg sodium, 0 g carbo., 0 g fiber, 4 g pro.*

PREP: **35 MINUTES**
BAKE: **10 MINUTES**
OVEN: **425°F**

16 servings	ingredients	32 servings
16	fresh or frozen large shrimp in shells	32
1 oz.	cream cheese, softened	2 oz.
2 Tbsp.	mayonnaise	¼ cup
1 tsp.	Dijon mustard	2 tsp.
⅛ tsp.	salt	¼ tsp.
1 6.5-oz. can	lump crabmeat, drained and flaked	2 6.5-oz. cans
2 Tbsp.	finely chopped green onion	¼ cup
2 Tbsp.	finely chopped roasted red sweet pepper	¼ cup

CHAPTER 2

Poultry

Here it is—the best of the bird. Whether you like chicken fried, grilled, stuffed, or roasted, this collection will bring chicken home to roost.

36

62

68

Chicken Pasta Casserole

A blanket of buttery-crisp, almond-studded panko cuddles this creamy concoction in crunchiness.

1. Preheat oven to 350°F. Cook pasta according to package directions; drain. Return pasta to pan.

2. Meanwhile, in a large skillet heat oil; add garlic and cook for 30 seconds. Season chicken with basil, salt, and pepper. Add chicken to the skillet; cook 3 minutes or until no pink remains. Remove from skillet. Add onion and sweet pepper to skillet; cook until tender. Stir in asparagus and cooked chicken. Remove from heat and set aside.

3. Stir cheese into pasta until melted. Stir in chicken mixture and half-and-half. Transfer to a 2-quart rectangular baking dish. In a small bowl combine bread crumbs, almonds, and butter; sprinkle over casserole.

4. Bake, uncovered, for 35 minutes or until heated through.

FOR 10 SERVINGS: Prepare using method above, except in Step 3 use a 3-quart rectangular baking dish.

PER SERVING 615 cal., 31 g total fat (16 g sat. fat), 116 mg chol., 531 mg sodium, 48 g carbo., 4 g fiber, 33 g pro.

PREP: 30 MINUTES
BAKE: 35 MINUTES
OVEN: 350°F

5 servings	ingredients	10 servings
8 oz.	dried bow tie pasta	1 lb.
2 Tbsp.	olive oil	¼ cup
6 cloves	garlic, minced	12 cloves
1 lb.	skinless, boneless chicken breast halves, cut into 1-inch pieces	2 lb.
1 tsp.	dried basil, crushed	2 tsp.
½ tsp.	salt	1 tsp.
¼ tsp.	black pepper	½ tsp.
½ cup	chopped onion	1 cup
½ cup	chopped red sweet pepper	1 cup
1 cup	frozen cut asparagus	2 cups
1 8-oz. container	cream cheese spread with chive and onion	2 8-oz. containers
¾ cup	half-and-half, light cream, or milk	1½ cups
½ cup	panko (Japanese-style bread crumbs)	1 cup
¼ cup	sliced almonds	½ cup
1 Tbsp.	butter, melted	2 Tbsp.

Creamy Chicken-Broccoli Bake

Even the kids will eat their broccoli when it's nestled in this creamy noodle bake.

PREP: 30 MINUTES
BAKE: 55 MINUTES
OVEN: 350°F

6 servings	ingredients	12 servings
	Nonstick cooking spray	
5 oz.	dried medium noodles	10 oz.
¾ lb.	skinless, boneless chicken breast, cut into bite-size pieces	1½ lb.
1½ cups	sliced fresh mushrooms	3 cups
½ cup	sliced green onions	1 cup
¼ cup	chopped red sweet pepper	½ cup
1 10.75-oz. can	condensed cream of broccoli soup	2 10.75-oz. cans
1 8-oz. carton	sour cream	2 8-oz. cartons
3 Tbsp.	chicken broth	⅓ cup
1 tsp.	dry mustard	2 tsp.
⅛ tsp.	black pepper	¼ tsp.
½ 16-oz. pkg.	frozen chopped broccoli, thawed and drained	1 16-oz. pkg.
¼ cup	fine dry bread crumbs	½ cup
1 Tbsp.	butter or margarine, melted	2 Tbsp.

1. Coat a 2-quart rectangular baking dish with nonstick cooking spray; set aside. Preheat oven to 350°F.

2. Cook noodles according to package directions; drain. Rinse with cold water; drain again.

3. Meanwhile, coat an unheated large skillet with nonstick cooking spray. Preheat over medium heat. Add chicken to hot skillet. Cook and stir about 3 minutes or until chicken is no longer pink. Transfer chicken to a large bowl.

4. Add mushrooms, green onions, and sweet pepper to skillet. Cook and stir until vegetables are tender. (If necessary, add 1 tablespoon vegetable oil to skillet.) Transfer vegetables to bowl with chicken. Stir in cream of broccoli soup, sour cream, broth, mustard, and black pepper. Gently stir in cooked noodles and broccoli.

5. Spoon chicken mixture into prepared dish. In a small bowl combine bread crumbs and melted butter; sprinkle over chicken mixture. Bake, covered, for 30 minutes. Uncover and bake about 25 minutes more or until heated through.

FOR 12 SERVINGS: Prepare using method above, except in Step 1 use a 3-quart baking dish.

PER SERVING 336 cal., 15 g total fat (8 g sat. fat), 79 mg chol., 515 mg sodium, 29 g carbo., 3 g fiber, 21 g pro.

Chicken and Gorgonzola Cheese

Make tonight special. Buttery blue cheese and Parmesan flavors make this plate of pasta perfect with a bottle of Pinot Grigio wine.

1. Sprinkle chicken with ¼ teaspoon of the salt and ¼ teaspoon of the pepper.

2. In a large nonstick skillet heat 1 tablespoon of the oil over medium-high heat. Add half the chicken; cook and stir until brown. Remove from skillet. Repeat with another 1 tablespoon oil and the remaining chicken; remove from skillet. Add the remaining 1 tablespoon oil and mushrooms. Cook for 5 to 8 minutes or until mushrooms are softened and liquid is evaporated, stirring occasionally.

3. Return chicken to skillet; stir in cream. Bring to boiling; reduce heat. Boil gently, uncovered, for 3 minutes. Stir in ½ cup of the Gorgonzola cheese, the Parmesan cheese, the remaining ¼ teaspoon salt, and the remaining ¼ teaspoon pepper. Cook and stir about 1 minute or until cheeses are melted.

4. Add chicken mixture, the remaining ½ cup Gorgonzola cheese, and parsley to hot cooked pasta; toss gently to combine.

FOR 12 SERVINGS: Prepare using method above, except in Step 1 use ½ teaspoon salt and ½ teaspoon pepper. In Step 2 heat 2 tablespoons oil; cook half of the chicken. Repeat with another 2 tablespoons oil and the remaining chicken. Use the remaining 2 tablespoons to cook the mushrooms. In Step 3 use 1 cup of Gorgonzola cheese, the Parmesan cheese, and the remaining ½ teaspoon salt and ½ teaspoon pepper. In Step 4 use the remaining 1 cup Gorgonzola cheese.

PER SERVING 800 cal., 48 g total fat (26 g sat. fat), 200 mg chol., 753 mg sodium, 47 g carbo., 2 g fiber, 45 g pro.

START TO FINISH: **30 MINUTES**

6 servings	ingredients	12 servings
1½ lb.	skinless, boneless chicken breast halves, cut crosswise into ½-inch slices	3 lb.
½ tsp.	salt	1 tsp.
½ tsp.	freshly ground black pepper	1 tsp.
3 Tbsp.	olive oil	6 Tbsp.
8 oz.	stemmed fresh cremini, shiitake, and/or button mushrooms, sliced	1 lb.
2 cups	whipping cream	4 cups
1 cup	crumbled Gorgonzola cheese	2 cups
⅔ cup	grated Parmesan cheese	1⅓ cups
¼ cup	snipped fresh parsley	½ cup
12 to 16 oz.	dried pasta, cooked and drained	24 to 32 oz.

Chicken and Olives

This is a perfect time to check out your supermarket's olive bar. Bring home some interesting olives and let them roll into this delicious dinner.

6 servings	ingredients	12 servings
12 to 16 oz.	dried pasta, cooked and drained	24 to 32 oz.
1 lb.	skinless, boneless chicken breast halves, cut into 1-inch pieces	2 lb.
1 large	onion, cut into thin wedges	2 large
2 cloves	garlic, minced	4 cloves
2 Tbsp.	olive oil	¼ cup
1 28-oz. can	Italian-style whole peeled tomatoes in puree	2 28-oz. cans
½ tsp.	coarsely ground black pepper	1 tsp.
¼ tsp.	salt	½ tsp.
½ cup	whipping cream	1 cup
1½ cups	large pimento-stuffed green olives and/or pitted Kalamata or other Italian olives, sliced	3 cups
½ cup	slivered fresh basil	1 cup
¼ cup	grated Parmesan cheese	½ cup

1. Cook pasta according to package directions. Drain. Cover and keep warm.

2. In a large skillet cook chicken, onion, and garlic in hot oil over medium-high heat for 5 to 7 minutes or until chicken is no longer pink, stirring occasionally. Meanwhile, place half of the tomatoes in a blender or food processor. Cover and blend or process until smooth. Snip the remaining tomatoes into bite-size pieces.

3. Stir pureed tomatoes, snipped tomatoes, pepper, and salt into chicken mixture. Bring to boiling; reduce heat. Boil gently, uncovered, for 2 minutes. Stir in cream. Boil gently, uncovered, for 3 minutes more, stirring occasionally. Stir in olives; heat through.

4. Top hot pasta with chicken mixture, basil, and cheese.

PER SERVING *499 cal., 20 g total fat (7 g sat. fat), 74 mg chol., 891 mg sodium, 53 g carbo., 5 g fiber, 28 g pro.*

Chicken, Macaroni, and Cheese

Monotone mac and cheese gets a splash of color with the addition of cherry tomatoes and fresh baby spinach. Slice a crusty baguette to serve alongside.

1. In a medium saucepan cook macaroni according to package directions, except do not add salt to the water; drain.

2. Meanwhile, coat an unheated large nonstick skillet with cooking spray. Preheat skillet over medium-high heat. Add chicken and onion to skillet. Cook for 4 to 6 minutes or until chicken is no longer pink and onion is tender, stirring frequently. (If onion browns too quickly, reduce heat to medium.) Remove skillet from heat. Stir in semisoft cheese until melted.

3. In a medium bowl whisk together milk and flour until smooth. Add all at once to chicken mixture. Cook and stir over medium heat until thickened and bubbly. Reduce heat to low. Stir in cheddar cheese until melted. Add cooked macaroni; cook and stir for 1 to 2 minutes or until heated through. Stir in spinach and top with cherry tomatoes. Serve immediately.

PER SERVING *369 cal., 12 g total fat (7 g sat. fat), 85 mg chol., 393 mg sodium, 33 g carbo., 4 g fiber, 33 g pro.*

START TO FINISH: **35 MINUTES**

5 servings	ingredients	10 servings
1½ cups	packaged dried multigrain or regular elbow macaroni	3 cups
	Nonstick cooking spray	
12 oz.	skinless, boneless chicken breast halves, cut into 1-inch pieces	24 oz.
¼ cup	finely chopped onion	½ cup
1 6.5-oz. pkg.	light semisoft cheese with garlic and herb	2 6.5-oz. pkgs.
1⅔ cups	fat-free milk	3⅓ cups
1 Tbsp.	all-purpose flour	2 Tbsp.
¾ cup	shredded reduced-fat cheddar cheese	1½ cups
2 cups	packaged fresh baby spinach	4 cups
1 cup	cherry tomatoes, quartered	2 cups

Prosciutto-Provolone Stuffed Chicken Breasts

Perched on a bed of Parmesan-garlic pasta, these Italian ham and cheese-stuffed rolls prove that elegant can be easy.

PREP: 45 MINUTES
BAKE: 12 MINUTES
OVEN: 400°F

4 servings	ingredients	8 servings
4	boneless, skinless chicken breast halves	8
⅛ tsp.	salt	¼ tsp.
⅛ tsp.	black pepper	¼ tsp.
8 thin slices	prosciutto	16 thin slices
8 slices	provolone cheese	16 slices
½ cup	lightly packed fresh basil leaves	1 cup
¼ cup	olive oil	½ cup
8 oz.	dried fettuccine or linguine	1 lb.
1 Tbsp.	butter	2 Tbsp.
4 cloves	garlic, chopped	8 cloves
2 cups	baby spinach	4 cups
1 cup	grated Parmesan cheese	2 cups
	Fresh basil leaves (optional)	

1. Preheat oven to 400°F. Place each chicken breast half between two pieces of plastic wrap. Using the flat side of a meat mallet, pound chicken lightly, working from the center to the edges until about ⅛ inch thick and the breast half is rectangular. Remove plastic wrap. Sprinkle both sides with the salt and pepper.

2. Lay 2 slices of the prosciutto, 2 slices of the provolone cheese, and a few basil leaves on each chicken piece. Fold in side edges; roll up from long edge, pressing firmly to seal in the filling. Secure each with a wooden toothpick.

3. In a large cast-iron or oven-going skillet heat half of the oil over medium-high heat. Add the chicken rolls. Cook about 6 minutes or until golden brown, turning to brown all sides. Transfer skillet to the oven and bake, uncovered, for 12 to 15 minutes or until chicken is no longer pink (170°F).

4. Meanwhile, cook pasta in lightly salted, boiling water according to package directions; drain. Return pasta to hot pan; cover and keep warm.

5. Remove chicken from skillet; keep warm. In the same skillet add the remaining 2 tablespoons of oil, the butter, and garlic. Cook and stir over medium heat for 1 minute. Remove skillet from heat. Add the drained pasta; toss to coat. Add spinach to skillet; toss with pasta. Sprinkle with half of the Parmesan cheese; toss to coat.

6. To serve, remove toothpicks from chicken; discard. Slice chicken rolls; arrange on the pasta. Serve with the remaining Parmesan cheese on the side. If desired, garnish with additional basil leaves.

PER SERVING *793 cal., 39 g total fat (13 g sat. fat), 127 mg chol., 1,246 mg sodium, 45 g carbo., 2 g fiber, 62 g pro.*

Sweet-and-Sour Baked Chicken

Who needs Chinese takeout? Do it home-style with tender chicken, a tumble of green peppers, and a pile of pineapple glistening in gingery orange sauce.

PREP: 25 MINUTES
BAKE: 30 MINUTES
OVEN: 350°F

4 servings	ingredients	8 servings
4	skinless, boneless chicken breast halves	8
	Salt and black pepper	
1 Tbsp.	vegetable oil	2 Tbsp.
½ 20-oz. can	pineapple chunks (juice pack), undrained	1 20-oz. can
½ cup	jellied cranberry sauce	1 cup
2 Tbsp.	cornstarch	¼ cup
2 Tbsp.	packed brown sugar	¼ cup
2 Tbsp.	rice vinegar or cider vinegar	¼ cup
2 Tbsp.	frozen orange juice concentrate, thawed	¼ cup
2 Tbsp.	dry sherry, chicken broth, or water	¼ cup
2 Tbsp.	soy sauce	¼ cup
¼ tsp.	ground ginger	½ tsp.
1 medium	green sweet peppers, cut in bite-size strips	2 medium

1. Preheat oven to 350°F. Lightly sprinkle chicken with salt and black pepper. In a large skillet heat oil over medium-high heat. Add chicken; cook about 4 minutes or until brown, turning once. (If necessary, brown chicken in batches.) Transfer chicken to an ungreased 2-quart rectangular baking dish. Drain pineapple, reserving ⅓ cup juice. Spoon pineapple chunks evenly over chicken; set aside.

2. For sauce, in a medium saucepan whisk together the reserved pineapple juice, cranberry sauce, cornstarch, brown sugar, vinegar, orange juice concentrate, sherry, soy sauce, and ginger. Cook and stir over medium heat until thickened and bubbly. Pour over chicken and pineapple in dish.

3. Bake, covered, for 25 minutes. Add sweet peppers, stirring gently to coat with sauce. Bake, uncovered, about 5 minutes more or until chicken is no longer pink (170°F).

FOR 8 SERVINGS: Prepare as above, except in Step 1 use a 3-quart baking dish and reserve ⅔ cup pineapple juice.

PER SERVING 354 cal., 5 g total fat (1 g sat. fat), 82 mg chol., 669 mg sodium, 37 g carbo., 2 g fiber, 34 g pro.

Grilled Chicken and Creamy Corn

If you're lucky enough to have leftovers, chop them up and roll them into a tomato-flavor wrap for tomorrow's lunch.

1. In a small bowl combine olive oil and paprika. Brush chicken and corn with oil mixture. Lightly sprinkle with salt and pepper.

2. For a charcoal grill, grill chicken on the rack of an uncovered grill directly over medium coals for 12 to 15 minutes or until chicken is no longer pink (170°F), turning once halfway through grilling. (For a gas grill, preheat grill. Reduce heat to medium. Place chicken on grill rack over heat. Cover and grill as above.)

3. With a sharp knife, carefully cut kernels from cob by firmly holding the corn at the top (using a kitchen towel to grip, if necessary) and slicing downward. Transfer kernels to a medium bowl; stir in sour cream. Season with additional salt and pepper. Stir in enough milk to make mixture creamy. Slice chicken breasts. Serve with corn and sprinkle with shredded basil.

PER SERVING 309 cal., 13 g total fat (4 g sat. fat), 89 mg chol., 238 mg sodium, 14 g carbo., 2 g fiber, 36 g pro.

START TO FINISH: **20 MINUTES**

4 servings	ingredients	8 servings
2 Tbsp.	olive oil	¼ cup
1 tsp.	smoked paprika	2 tsp.
4	skinless, boneless chicken breast halves	8
3 ears	sweet corn, husks and silks removed	6 ears
	Salt	
	Black pepper	
⅓ cup	sour cream	⅔ cup
	Milk	
¼ cup	shredded fresh basil	½ cup

Chicken and Pasta Primavera

Healthful carrots, zucchini, and corn make this yummy toss not only a creamy bowl of carbohydrate heaven, but a serving of vegetables as well.

1. Cook pasta according to package directions, adding carrots, zucchini, and corn to the water with pasta; drain. Return pasta and vegetables to saucepan; add chicken. (If the chicken has been refrigerated, place it in a colander. Pour pasta, vegetables, and cooking liquid over chicken to warm it; drain and return to saucepan.)

2. Meanwhile, in a medium saucepan stir together broth, cornstarch, lemon peel, and basil. Cook and stir over medium heat until thickened and bubbly. Cook and stir for 2 minutes more. Remove from heat. Stir in sour cream and mustard. Pour over pasta mixture, tossing gently to coat. Sprinkle with cheese. Serve immediately.

PER SERVING *334 cal., 10 g total fat (4 g sat. fat), 98 mg chol., 547 mg sodium, 34 g carbo., 3 g fiber, 27 g pro.*

START TO FINISH: **25 MINUTES**

6 servings	ingredients	12 servings
1 9-oz. pkg.	refrigerated spinach or plain fettuccine	2 9-oz. pkgs.
1 cup	thinly sliced carrots	2 cups
1 medium	zucchini, halved lengthwise and thinly sliced	2 medium
¾ cup	frozen whole kernel corn	1½ cups
3 cups	shredded cooked chicken	6 cups
1½ cups	chicken broth	3 cups
4 tsp.	cornstarch	3 Tbsp.
2 tsp.	finely shredded lemon peel	4 tsp.
1 tsp.	dried basil, crushed	2 tsp.
½ cup	sour cream	1 cup
2 Tbsp.	Dijon mustard	¼ cup
	Finely shredded Parmesan cheese	

Chicken Linguine with Pesto Sauce

Busy weeknight activities call for creative kitchen helpers. Tonight's trusty timesavers—purchased pesto, ready-made Alfredo sauce, and a hot-off-the-rotisserie deli chicken bring dinner to the table in a hurry.

START TO FINISH: **20 MINUTES**

4 servings	ingredients	8 servings
8 oz.	dried linguine	1 lb.
1 10-oz. pkg.	frozen broccoli, cauliflower, and carrots	2 10-oz. pkgs.
1 10-oz. container	refrigerated Alfredo pasta sauce or 1 cup bottled Alfredo sauce	2 10-oz. containers
⅓ cup	purchased basil pesto	⅔ cup
¼ cup	milk	½ cup
½ a 2- to 2½-lb.	deli-roasted chicken	1 2- to 2½-lb.
	Milk (optional)	
	Grated Parmesan cheese	

1. In a 4- or 5-quart Dutch oven, cook pasta according to package directions, adding vegetables during the last 5 minutes of cooking; drain. Return pasta and vegetables to Dutch oven.

2. While pasta is cooking, in a small bowl combine Alfredo sauce, pesto, and milk; set aside. Remove and discard skin from chicken. Pull meat from bones, discarding bones. Chop or shred meat.

3. Add chicken to pasta and vegetables in Dutch oven. Add sauce mixture, tossing gently to coat. Heat through over medium-low heat. If desired, stir in additional milk to reach desired consistency. Divide among 4 dinner plates. Sprinkle Parmesan cheese on each serving.

PER SERVING *801 cal., 48 g total fat (4 g sat. fat), 109 mg chol., 546 mg sodium, 54 g carbo., 3 g fiber, 37 g pro.*

Chicken with Orzo

Quick-cooking orzo joins deli chicken to make Mediterranean-style mealtime magic.

1. Cook orzo according to package directions; drain. Return orzo to saucepan.

2. Add spinach, half the feta cheese, and the lemon peel to orzo in saucepan, tossing to mix. Divide orzo mixture among 4 dinner plates. Arrange chicken pieces and tomato wedges on orzo mixture. Sprinkle with remaining feta cheese.

FOR 8 SERVINGS: Prepare using method above, except in Step 2 use 8 dinner plates.

PER SERVING *528 cal., 19 g total fat (7 g sat. fat), 112 mg chol., 267 mg sodium, 45 g carbo., 3 g fiber, 41 g pro.*

START **TO FINISH: 15 MINUTES**

4 servings	ingredients	8 servings
8 oz.	dried orzo pasta	1 lb.
2 cups	shredded fresh spinach leaves	4 cups
½ cup	crumbled feta cheese	1 cup
1 tsp.	finely shredded lemon peel	2 tsp.
1 2- to 2½-lb.	hot deli-roasted chicken, cut into serving-size pieces	2 2- to 2½-lb.
1 medium	tomato, cut in wedges	2 medium

Easy Chicken and Dumplings

Sure, your grandma made dumplings from scratch—but if she would have been able to pop open a can of biscuits to get the job done, she probably would have.

PREP: 25 MINUTES
COOK: 15 MINUTES

4 servings	ingredients	8 servings
1 2- to 2½-lb.	deli-roasted chicken	2 2- to 2½-lb.
1 16-oz. pkg.	frozen mixed vegetables	2 16-oz. pkgs.
1¼ cups	reduced-sodium chicken broth or water	2½ cups
1 10.75-oz. can	reduced-fat, reduced-sodium condensed cream of chicken soup	2 10.75-oz. cans
½ tsp.	dried Italian seasoning, crushed	1 tsp.
⅛ tsp.	black pepper	¼ tsp.
1 16.3-oz. can	flaky layers buttermilk refrigerated biscuits	1 16.3-oz. can

1. Remove and discard skin from chicken. Pull meat from bones, discarding bones. Chop or shred meat.

2. In a large saucepan combine chicken, vegetables, broth, soup, Italian seasoning, and pepper. Bring to boiling; reduce heat. Cover and simmer about 15 minutes or until vegetables are tender.

3. Meanwhile, remove biscuits from package. Bake according to package directions.

4. To serve, place the bottom of a biscuit in each bowl. Spoon chicken mixture on biscuit then top with biscuit top.

FOR 4 SERVINGS: Prepare using method above, except use 4 biscuits and freeze 4 biscuits for later.

PER SERVING *650 cal., 30 g total fat (8 g sat. fat), 107 mg chol., 1,399 mg sodium, 57 g carbo., 5 g fiber, 42 g pro.*

Tetrazzini Primavera

Tag this page with a sticky note—you'll want to remember this recipe next Thanksgiving when you're looking for a yummy way to utilize leftover turkey.

PREP: **40 MINUTES**   BAKE: **35 MINUTES**
STAND: **5 MINUTES**   OVEN: **350°F**

6 servings	ingredients	12 servings
	Nonstick cooking spray	
8 oz.	dried whole wheat linguine or spaghetti, broken in half	1 lb.
1 lb.	broccoli, trimmed and cut into 1-inch pieces	2 lb.
2 Tbsp.	butter	¼ cup
3 medium	red and/or yellow sweet peppers, stemmed, seeded, and cut into 1-inch pieces	6 medium
2 cloves	garlic, minced	4 cloves
¼ cup	all-purpose flour	½ cup
1 14-oz. can	reduced-sodium chicken broth	2 14-oz. cans
¾ cup	fat-free milk	1½ cups
½ cup	light sour cream	1 cup
3 cups	shredded cooked turkey or chicken	6 cups
¾ cup	shredded white cheddar cheese	1½ cups
1 cup	soft bread crumbs	2 cups
1 Tbsp.	snipped fresh parsley	2 Tbsp.
1 tsp.	finely shredded lemon peel	2 tsp.
1 Tbsp.	olive oil	2 Tbsp.

1. Preheat oven to 350°F. Coat a 3-quart casserole with cooking spray; set aside.

2. In a Dutch oven cook linguine according to package directions, adding broccoli for the last 2 minutes of cooking time. Drain. Return linguine and broccoli to Dutch oven.

3. Meanwhile, for sauce, in a large skillet melt butter over medium heat. Add sweet peppers and garlic; cook about 5 minutes or just until peppers are tender, stirring occasionally. Stir in flour, ¼ teaspoon *salt*, and ⅛ teaspoon *black pepper* until combined. Add broth and milk all at once. Cook and stir until thickened and bubbly. Stir in sour cream.

4. Add sauce, turkey, and cheese to linguine mixture; toss to coat. Spoon into prepared casserole. Bake, covered, for 25 minutes. Meanwhile, for the bread crumb topping, in a small bowl toss together soft bread crumbs, parsley, lemon peel, and olive oil.

5. Sprinkle bread crumb topping on turkey and pasta mixture. Bake, uncovered, for 10 to 15 minutes more or until heated through and topper is lightly browned. Let stand for 5 minutes before serving.

FOR 12 SERVINGS: Prepare using method above, except in Step 1 use two 3-quart casseroles. In Step 3 use ½ teaspoon salt and ¼ teaspoon black pepper. In Step 4 divide turkey and linguine mixture evenly between the two prepared casseroles.

PER SERVING *473 cal., 17 g total fat (11 g sat. fat), 84 mg chol., 515 mg sodium, 46 g carbo., 6 g fiber, 35 g pro.*

Spicy Egg-Stuffed Peppers

This economical dish is raring to go on breakfast-for-supper night. If your family goes for a lot of spicy kick, bake the egg mixture in Poblano chile peppers.

1. Half peppers lengthwise, leaving stem ends intact. Remove and discard seeds and ribs. (If using poblano peppers, cut off a thin slice from the side of each and discard seeds.) In a large saucepan or pot, cook peppers in a large amount of boiling water for 3 to 5 minutes or just until tender. Invert pepper halves on paper towels to drain.

2. In a large skillet heat oil over medium heat. Add zucchini, onion, and chopped sausage; cook about 3 minutes or just until zucchini is tender, stirring occasionally. Remove zucchini mixture from skillet; set aside.

3. Preheat oven to 325°F. In a medium bowl whisk together eggs and milk. Add egg mixture to hot skillet. Cook over medium heat, without stirring, until mixture begins to set on the bottom and around the edges. With a spatula or large spoon, lift and fold the partially cooked egg mixture so the uncooked portion flows underneath. Continue cooking over medium heat for 2 to 3 minutes or until egg mixture is cooked through, but still glossy and moist. Fold in vegetable mixture.

4. In a 2-quart rectangular baking dish, arrange peppers cut sides up. Spoon zucchini mixture into peppers. Sprinkle with cheese. Bake for 10 to 15 minutes or until cheese is melted and filling is heated through.

FOR 8 SERVINGS: Prepare using method above, except in Step 4 use a 3-quart rectangular baking dish.

*TIP: If using Italian chicken sausage or turkey sausage, add 1 fresh jalapeño chile pepper, seeded and finely chopped, to skillet with the sausage (see tip, page 18).

PER SERVING 197 cal., 11 g total fat (4 g sat. fat), 235 mg chol., 285 mg sodium, 11 g carbo., 3 g fiber, 14 g pro.

PREP: **35 MINUTES**
BAKE: **10 MINUTES**
OVEN: **325°F**

4 servings	ingredients	8 servings
4 medium	yellow, red, and/or green sweet peppers and/or medium fresh poblano chile peppers	8 medium
2 tsp.	olive oil	4 tsp.
1 cup	chopped zucchini	2 cups
½ cup	chopped onion	1 cup
1 3-oz. link	cooked habeñero-chile chicken sausage or chicken sweet Italian sausage* or 3 ounces cooked smoked turkey sausage,* chopped	2 3-oz. links
4	eggs	8
2 Tbsp.	fat-free milk	¼ cup
¼ cup	shredded Monterey Jack cheese	½ cup

Curried Chicken Skillet

The juicy sweetness of fresh mango balances this spicy curry dish. When selecting mangoes, choose plump fruit blushed with reddish-orange. The best mangoes are fragrant and firm to the touch, but give slightly when pressed with the thumb.

START TO FINISH: **15 MINUTES**

2 servings	ingredients	4 servings
	Nonstick cooking spray	
⅓ cup	chopped onion	⅔ cup
1 tsp.	curry powder	2 tsp.
⅔ cup	water	1⅓ cups
⅓ cup	quick-cooking couscous	⅔ cup
1 cup	cubed cooked chicken breast	2 cups
⅓ cup	loose-pack frozen peas	⅔ cup
¼ cup	fat-free mayonnaise or salad dressing	½ cup
¼ cup	chopped red sweet pepper	½ cup
2 Tbsp.	bottled mango chutney	¼ cup
	Mango, seeded, peeled, and chopped (optional)	

1. Lightly coat an unheated large skillet with cooking spray. Preheat skillet over medium heat. Add onion; cook and stir for 4 to 5 minutes or until onion is crisp-tender. Stir in curry powder; cook for 1 minute. Add the water and couscous to skillet; bring to boiling. Remove from heat.

2. Stir in chicken, peas, mayonnaise, sweet pepper, and chutney; cover and let stand for 5 minutes. Return to medium heat until heated through.

3. Divide curried chicken among 2 dinner plates. Top with mango, if desired.

FOR 4 SERVINGS: Prepare using method above, except in Step 3 divide chicken mixture among 4 dinner plates.

PER SERVING *303 cal., 3 g total fat (1 g sat. fat), 59 mg chol., 365 mg sodium, 39 g carbo., 3 g fiber, 27 g pro.*

Kalamata Lemon Chicken

Round out this Greek chicken dinner with a bed of mixed greens scattered with feta cheese, grape tomatoes, and sliced cucumbers dressed with a drizzle of lemon vinaigrette.

1. Preheat oven to 400°F. In a 4-quart Dutch oven heat oil over medium-high heat. Add chicken; cook about 5 minutes or until brown, turning once. Remove chicken from Dutch oven. Add broth, orzo, olives, lemon wedges, lemon juice, Greek seasoning, salt, and pepper to Dutch oven. Return chicken to Dutch oven.

2. Bake, covered, about 35 minutes or until chicken is tender and no longer pink (180°F). If desired, sprinkle with fresh oregano and serve in shallow bowls with additional hot broth.

FOR 8 SERVINGS: Prepare using method above, except in Step 1 use a 3-quart rectangular baking dish.

PER SERVING 304 cal., 10 g total fat (2 g sat. fat), 95 mg chol., 830 mg sodium, 25 g carbo., 2 g fiber, 27 g pro.

PREP: **10 MINUTES**
BAKE: **35 MINUTES**
OVEN: **400°F**

4 servings	ingredients	8 servings
1 Tbsp.	olive oil	2 Tbsp.
1 lb.	skinless, boneless chicken thighs	2 lb.
1 14-oz. can	chicken broth	2 14-oz. cans
⅔ cup	dried orzo	1⅓ cups
½ cup	drained pitted Kalamata olives	1 cup
½ of a	lemon, cut in wedges or chunks	1
1 Tbsp.	lemon juice	2 Tbsp.
1 tsp.	dried Greek seasoning or dried oregano, crushed	2 tsp.
¼ tsp.	salt	½ tsp.
¼ tsp.	black pepper	½ tsp.
	Fresh snipped oregano (optional)	
	Hot chicken broth (optional)	

Lemon-Herb Chicken with Ricotta Salata

Sop up the bird's savory lemon and herb juices with chunks of ciabatta or focaccia bread.

1. For rub, in a small bowl combine 1 teaspoon of the lemon peel, the basil, rosemary, garlic, salt, and pepper. Sprinkle rub evenly over chicken; rub in with your fingers. Place chicken in a 3½- or 4-quart slow cooker. Pour broth over chicken.

2. Cover and cook on low-heat setting for 4½ to 5 hours. Transfer chicken to a serving platter.

3. Skim fat from cooking liquid. Spoon some of the cooking liquid over chicken; discard the remaining liquid. Sprinkle chicken with ricotta salata, parsley, and the remaining lemon peel. If desired, serve with rice.

FOR 10 SERVINGS: Prepare recipe using method above, except in Step 1 use 2 teaspoons of the lemon peel. Place chicken in a 5- or 6-quart slow cooker.

PER SERVING 245 cal., 8 g total fat (1 g sat. fat), 132 mg chol., 617 mg sodium, 1 g carbo., 0 g fiber, 40 g pro.

PREP: 20 MINUTES
COOK: 4½ HOURS (LOW)

5 servings	ingredients	10 servings
2 tsp.	finely shredded lemon peel	4 tsp.
1 tsp.	dried basil, crushed	2 tsp.
1 tsp.	dried rosemary, crushed	2 tsp.
2 cloves	garlic, minced	4 cloves
½ tsp.	salt	1 tsp.
¼ tsp.	black pepper	½ tsp.
4 lb.	chicken thighs and/or drumsticks, skinned	8 lb.
½ cup	reduced-sodium chicken broth	1 cup
½ cup	crumbled ricotta salata	1 cup
2 Tbsp.	coarsely snipped fresh parsley	¼ cup
	Cooked rice (optional)	

Tomato and Olive Chicken

Make sure to have an ovenproof heavy skillet for this one-dish meal. If your skillet does not have a metal handle, wrap its synthetic handle with aluminum foil for heat protection.

PREP: 20 MINUTES
BAKE: 25 MINUTES
OVEN: 400°F

4 servings	ingredients	8 servings
3 lb.	skinless chicken thighs (bone in)	6 lb.
	Salt	
	Black pepper	
1 Tbsp.	olive oil	2 Tbsp.
1 cup	chicken broth	2 cups
1 cup	dried orzo (rosamarina) pasta	2 cups
8	roma tomatoes, halved and seeded	16
½ cup	pitted Kalamata olives	1 cup
	Fresh basil leaves	

1. Preheat oven to 400°F. Lightly season chicken with salt and black pepper. In a very large oven-going skillet heat oil over medium-high heat. Add chicken thighs, meaty side down, and cook for 10 minutes or until brown, turning halfway through cooking. Remove chicken from skillet; discard pan drippings.

2. Add broth to skillet; bring to boiling. Stir in orzo. Return chicken to skillet, meaty side up, and add tomatoes and olives.

3. Baked, covered, about 25 minutes or until chicken is no longer pink (180°F) and orzo is tender. Sprinkle with basil.

PER SERVING *796 cal., 46 g total fat (12 g sat. fat), 225 mg chol., 752 mg sodium, 40 g carbo., 4 g fiber, 54 g pro.*

Parisian Chicken Salad

Light and lovely, this beauty is ready for a spring fling.

1. Place chicken in a resealable plastic bag set in a shallow dish. For marinade, combine orange peel, the ⅓ cup orange juice, the 4 cloves garlic, honey, and thyme. Pour over chicken; seal bag. Marinate in the refrigerator for 6 to 8 hours, turning bag occasionally.

2. Drain chicken, discarding marinade. Place chicken on the unheated rack of a broiler pan. Season with half the salt and half the pepper. Broil 4 to 5 inches from heat for 12 to 15 minutes or until chicken is no longer pink (170°F), turning once halfway through broiling.

3. Meanwhile, for dressing, in a screw-top jar combine olive oil, vinegar, the 2 tablespoons orange juice, the 2 cloves garlic, shallot, and remaining salt and pepper. Cover and shake well.

4. Divide greens among 4 dinner plates. Top with sweet pepper slices. Slice chicken crosswise. Arrange chicken and orange sections on greens. Drizzle with dressing.

FOR 8 SERVINGS: Prepare using method above, except in Step 1 for the marinade combine orange peel, ⅔ cup orange juice, the 8 cloves garlic, honey, and thyme. In Step 3 for the dressing, in a screw top jar combine olive oil, vinegar, the ¼ cup orange juice, the 4 cloves garlic, shallot, and remaining salt and pepper. In Step 4 use 8 dinner plates.

PER SERVING 305 cal., 17 g total fat (3 g sat. fat), 59 mg chol., 261 mg sodium, 16 g carbo., 1 g fiber, 23 g pro.

PREP: **25 MINUTES**
MARINATE: **6 HOURS**
BROIL: **6 MINUTES**

4 servings	ingredients	8 servings
4	skinless, boneless chicken breast halves	8
2 tsp.	finely shredded orange peel	4 tsp.
⅓ cup	orange juice	⅔ cup
4 cloves	garlic, minced	8 cloves
2 Tbsp.	honey	¼ cup
1½ tsp.	dried thyme, crushed	1 Tbsp.
½ tsp.	salt	1 tsp.
¼ tsp.	black pepper	½ tsp.
¼ cup	olive oil	½ cup
2 Tbsp.	white wine vinegar	¼ cup
2 Tbsp.	orange juice	¼ cup
2 cloves	garlic, minced	4 cloves
1½ tsp.	finely chopped shallot	1 Tbsp.
4 cups	torn baby salad greens	8 cups
1 medium	yellow sweet pepper, thinly sliced	2 medium
2 medium	oranges, peeled and sectioned	4 medium

Southwestern Chicken and Black Bean Salad

Filled with a Tex-Mex fiesta of family-friendly flavors, this salad will even bring fussy kids to the table. If you top it with a double dose of tortilla chips, they just might clean their plates.

4 servings	ingredients	8 servings
10 cups	torn romaine lettuce leaves	20 cups
1 15-oz. can	black beans, rinsed and drained	2 15-oz. cans
1½ cups	chopped cooked chicken or turkey	3 cups
1½ cups	red and/or yellow cherry tomatoes, halved	3 cups
½ cup	bottled light Caesar salad dressing	1 cup
2 tsp.	chili powder	4 tsp.
½ tsp.	ground cumin	1 tsp.
½ cup	broken tortilla chips	1 cup
2 Tbsp.	snipped fresh cilantro or parsley	¼ cup
	Fresh cilantro sprigs (optional)	

1. In a large bowl combine romaine, black beans, chicken, and tomatoes.

2. For dressing, in a small bowl whisk together salad dressing, chili powder, and cumin. Pour dressing over salad; toss gently to coat. Sprinkle with tortilla chips and snipped cilantro. If desired, garnish with cilantro sprigs.

PER SERVING *295 cal., 10 g total fat (1 g sat. fat), 55 mg chol., 913 mg sodium, 26 g carbo., 9 g fiber, 27 g pro.*

Chicken-Rice Salad

Nutty-flavor garbanzo beans add an additional protein punch to this Mediterranean-style main dish salad.

1. In a medium saucepan combine rice and the water. Bring to boiling; reduce heat. Cover and simmer for 15 minutes or until the water is absorbed. Place rice in a colander; rinse with cold water. Drain well.

2. In a large bowl combine roasted red peppers, garbanzo beans, olives, and green onions. Drain artichoke hearts, reserving marinade. Chop artichokes; add to roasted red pepper mixture along with cooked rice; set aside.

3. Cut chicken into bite-size strips. Sprinkle with chili powder and rosemary. In a large nonstick skillet cook chicken in 1 tablespoon reserved artichoke marinade over medium heat for 3 to 4 minutes or until no longer pink.

4. Add chicken to rice mixture along with remaining artichoke marinade and feta cheese. Toss gently to combine. Cover and chill for 4 to 24 hours.

FOR 12 SERVINGS: Prepare using method above, except in Step 3 cook chicken in 2 tablespoons reserved artichoke marinade.

PER SERVING 264 cal., 8 g total fat (2 g sat. fat), 38 mg chol., 376 mg sodium, 33 g carbo., 2 g fiber, 16 g pro.

PREP: 35 MINUTES
COOK: 18 MINUTES
CHILL: 4 HOURS

6 servings	ingredients	12 servings
1 cup	uncooked long grain rice	2 cups
2 cups	water	4 cups
½ of a 7.5-oz. jar	roasted red sweet peppers, drained and chopped	1 7.5-oz. jar
½ cup	canned garbanzo beans (chickpeas), drained	1 cup
1 2.25-oz. can	sliced pitted ripe olives, drained	2 2.25-oz. cans
¼ cup	thinly sliced green onions	½ cup
1 6-oz. jar	marinated artichoke hearts	2 6-oz. jars
12 oz.	skinless, boneless chicken breasts	24 oz.
2 tsp.	chili powder	4 tsp.
½ tsp.	dried rosemary, crushed	1 tsp.
½ cup	crumbled feta cheese with basil and tomato or crumbled plain feta	1 cup

Berry Chicken Salad

Juicy red pears and beautiful blackberries put this salad on the menu for sultry summer evenings.

PREP: **30 MINUTES**
MARINATE: **1 HOUR**   GRILL: **12 MINUTES**

4 servings	ingredients	8 servings
½ cup	orange juice	1 cup
¼ cup	lime juice	½ cup
¼ cup	lemon juice	½ cup
1 Tbsp.	olive oil	2 Tbsp.
1 tsp.	chopped fresh basil	2 tsp.
4	skinless, boneless chicken breast halves	8
3 cups	fresh blackberries	6 cups
¼ cup	red wine vinegar	½ cup
3 Tbsp.	sugar	6 Tbsp.
1 tsp.	Dijon mustard	2 tsp.
¼ tsp.	dried oregano, crushed	½ tsp.
½ cup	olive oil	1 cup
1 8-oz. pkg.	Mediterranean mixed salad greens	2 8-oz. pkgs.
2 medium	pears, cored and thinly sliced	4 medium
¾ cup	crumbled feta cheese	1½ cups

1. For marinade, in a small bowl combine orange juice, lime juice, lemon juice, the 1 tablespoon oil, basil, ½ teaspoon *salt*, and ¼ teaspoon *black pepper*. Place chicken in a resealable plastic bag set in a shallow dish. Pour marinade over chicken; seal bag. Marinate in the refrigerator for 1 to 4 hours, turning bag occasionally.

2. For dressing, in a blender combine 1 cup of the blackberries, vinegar, sugar, mustard, oregano, ¼ teaspoon *salt*, and ¼ teaspoon *black pepper*. Cover and blend until smooth. With blender running, add the ½ cup oil in a thin steady stream until well combined. Transfer dressing to serving container. Cover and chill until serving time.

3. Drain chicken, discarding marinade. For a charcoal grill, place chicken on the rack of an uncovered grill directly over medium coals. Grill for 12 to 15 minutes or until chicken is no longer pink (170°F), turning once halfway through grilling. (For a gas grill, preheat grill. Reduce heat to medium. Place chicken on grill rack over heat. Cover; grill as above.)

4. Slice chicken crosswise. Divide greens among 4 dinner plates. Top with chicken, pears, and remaining blackberries. Top each salad with some of the dressing and feta cheese. Pass remaining dressing.

FOR 8 SERVINGS: Prepare recipe using method above, except in Step 1 combine orange juice, lime juice, lemon juice, the 2 tablespoons oil, basil, 1 teaspoon *salt*, and ½ teaspoon *black pepper*. In Step 2 in a blender combine 2 cups of the blackberries, vinegar, sugar, mustard, oregano, ½ teaspoon *salt*, and ½ teaspoon *black pepper*. In Step 4 use 8 dinner plates.

PER SERVING 603 cal., 35 g total fat (7 g sat. fat), 101 mg chol., 427 mg sodium, 36 g carbo., 9 g fiber, 38 g pro.

Smoked Chicken and Prosciutto Panini

To make homemade garlic oil for brushing on your panini, simply sauté 4 garlic cloves with ½ cup olive oil in a small saucepan over medium heat until fragrant. Store at room temperature.

1. For spread, in a food processor or blender combine mayonnaise, ¼ cup roasted peppers, and garlic. Cover and blend or process until nearly smooth.

2. Cut each roll in half horizontally; spread cut sides of rolls with spread. Layer 4 roasted peppers (if desired), chicken, prosciutto, cheese, and mesclun on roll bottoms. Replace tops. If desired, brush outsides of sandwiches with oil.

3. Preheat an electric sandwich press, a covered indoor grill, a grill pan, or a 12-inch skillet. Place sandwiches, half at a time if necessary, in the sandwich press or indoor grill. Cover and cook about 6 minutes or until rolls are lightly toasted and cheese is melted. (If using a grill pan or skillet, place sandwiches in pan. Weight sandwiches down with a heavy skillet or a pie plate containing a can of vegetables. Cook about 2 minutes or until rolls are lightly toasted. Turn sandwiches over, weight down, and cook about 2 minutes more or until rolls are lightly toasted and cheese is melted.)

PER SANDWICH 842 cal., 49 g total fat (17 g sat. fat), 111 mg chol., 2,465 mg sodium, 59 g carbo., 4 g fiber, 38 g pro.

PREP: **25 MINUTES**
GRILL: **6 MINUTES PER BATCH**

4 servings	ingredients	8 servings
½ cup	mayonnaise	1 cup
¼ cup	bottled roasted red sweet pepper, drained and patted dry with paper towels	½ cup
1 clove	garlic, quartered	2 cloves
4	soft French-style or sourdough rolls (about 7×3 inches)	8
4	bottled roasted red sweet peppers drained (optional)	8
8 oz.	thinly sliced smoked chicken or turkey	1 lb.
2 oz.	thinly sliced prosciutto	4 oz.
8 oz.	sliced provolone or mozzarella cheese	1 lb.
1 cup	mesclun or baby lettuce	2 cups
	Garlic-flavor oil (optional)	

Turkey Saltimbocca

Saltimbocca means "jump in the mouth."

4 servings	ingredients	8 servings
¼ cup	all-purpose flour	½ cup
½ tsp.	salt	1 tsp.
½ tsp.	dried sage, crushed	1 tsp.
¼ tsp.	black pepper	½ tsp.
4	turkey cutlets	8
2 Tbsp.	vegetable oil	¼ cup
4 slices	cooked ham	8 slices
4 slices	fontina or Swiss cheese	8 slices
¼ cup	dry white wine	½ cup
¼ cup	reduced-sodium chicken broth	½ cup
2 Tbsp.	snipped fresh parsley (optional)	¼ cup

1. In a shallow dish combine flour, salt, sage, and pepper. Set aside.

2. Place each turkey cutlet between two pieces of plastic wrap. Using the flat side of a meat mallet, pound turkey lightly, working from the center to the edges to about ¼ inch thick. Remove plastic wrap. Dip cutlets into flour mixture, turning to coat both sides; shake off excess.

3. In an extra-large nonstick skillet heat oil over medium-high heat. Add cutlets; cook about 2 minutes or until brown on bottom. Turn cutlets; top each with one slice of the ham and one slice of the cheese. Add wine and broth; cook about 2 minutes more or until cheese is melted and sauce is thickened.

4. Transfer cutlets to a serving platter. Spoon pan drippings over cutlets. If desired, garnish with parsley.

PER SERVING 282 cal., 14 g total fat (4 g sat. fat), 66 mg chol., 774 mg sodium, 7 g carbo., 1 g fiber, 28 g pro.

Turkey, Pear, and Cheese Salad

Whichever variety of pears you choose—Bartlett, Anjou, Forelle, or Bosc—pick pears neither too firm or too soft. Perfect pears will give slightly at their stem ends when pressed with a finger.

1. Bias slice the turkey crosswise into 1-inch thick slices. Flatten slightly with the palm of your hand and season with salt and pepper. Brush with about half the honey mustard.

2. In a 12-inch skillet heat 2 tablespoons of the oil over medium-high heat. Add turkey in an even layer; cook 2 to 3 minutes on each side or until browned. Scatter pears on the turkey. Top each piece of turkey with a half slice of cheese. Reduce heat to medium-low. Cover and cook 3 to 4 minutes or until cheese is melted and pears are warm.

3. Place 2 cups of arugula on each of 4 serving plates; divide turkey and pears on arugula. Whisk remaining mustard, oil and the vinegar into pan juices; cook 30 seconds. Drizzle over each serving. Sprinkle with freshly ground pepper, if desired.

FOR 8 SERVINGS: Prepare using method above, except use 8 serving plates in Step 3.

PER SERVING 410 cal., 22 g total fat (7 g sat. fat), 90 mg chol., 480 mg sodium, 16 g carbo., 3 g fiber, 36 g pro.

START TO FINISH: **25 MINUTES**

4 servings	ingredients	8 servings
1 lb.	turkey tenderloins	2 lb.
	Salt and black pepper	
1 Tbsp.	honey mustard	2 Tbsp.
¼ cup	olive oil	½ cup
2	pears, cored and sliced	4
4 slices	provolone cheese, halved	8 slices
5 oz.	arugula	10 oz.
2 Tbsp.	cider vinegar	¼ cup
	Freshly ground pepper (optional)	

Turkey Reuben Loaf

This sandwich is a great traveler, which makes it a tasty treat for picnics, potlucks, or tailgating.

1. Preheat oven to 400°F. For sauce, in a small bowl combine mayonnaise, pickle relish, and ketchup. In another bowl combine cabbage, vinegar, and caraway seeds.

2. Slice bread lengthwise. Hollow out some of the bread; reserve for making crumbs. Spread some of the sauce on cut sides of bread; reserve remaining for serving. Arrange half the cheese slices on bottom half of bread. Top with cabbage mixture, turkey, and remaining cheese. Top with bread; wrap tightly in foil and place on baking sheet. Bake for 10 minutes. Carefully unwrap and bake 2 to 3 minutes more until bread is crisp and cheese is melted.

3. To serve, cut loaf in slices with a sharp serrated knife. Pass remaining sauce.

PER SERVING 640 cal., 40 g total fat (13 g sat. fat), 85 mg chol., 931 mg sodium, 37 g carbo., 5 g fiber, 31 g pro.

START TO FINISH: **30 MINUTES** OVEN: **400°F**

4 servings	ingredients	8 servings
½ cup	mayonnaise	1 cup
¼ cup	pickle relish	½ cup
1 Tbsp.	ketchup	2 Tbsp.
2 cups	shredded cabbage	4 cups
2 tsp.	vinegar	4 tsp.
1 tsp.	caraway seeds	2 tsp.
½	unsliced oblong loaf of bread	1
6 oz.	Havarti cheese, sliced	12 oz.
8 oz.	cooked turkey, sliced or chopped	1 lb.

Turkey and Sweet Potato Shepherd's Pies

These adorable personal pies give comfort food a new twist while the sweet potato topping brings superfood status to a simple dish.

1. Preheat oven to 375°F. In a medium saucepan cook sweet potatoes and garlic, covered in enough lightly salted boiling water to cover for 15 to 20 minutes or until tender; drain. Mash with a potato masher or beat with an electric mixer on low. Gradually add milk and salt, mashing or beating to make potato mixture light and fluffy. Cover and keep warm.

2. Meanwhile, in a large skillet cook turkey and onion over medium heat until meat is brown, stirring with a wooden spoon to break up turkey as it cooks. Drain, if needed. Stir in zucchini, carrots, corn, and the water. Bring to boiling; reduce heat. Simmer, covered, for 5 to 10 minutes or until vegetables are tender.

3. Add tomato sauce, Worcestershire sauce, snipped sage, and pepper to turkey mixture; heat through. Divide turkey mixture among 4 ungreased 10-ounce ramekins, spreading evenly. Spoon mashed sweet potato mixture in mounds onto turkey mixture.

4. Bake, uncovered, for 20 to 25 minutes or until heated through. If desired, garnish with fresh sage leaves.

FOR 8 SERVINGS: Prepare using method above, except in Step 3 use 8 ungreased 10-ounce ramekins.

PER SERVING 268 cal., 1 g total fat (0 g sat. fat), 42 mg chol., 824 mg sodium, 41 g carbo., 7 g fiber, 24 g pro.

PREP: 40 MINUTES
BAKE: 20 MINUTES
OVEN: 375°F

4 servings	ingredients	8 servings
1½ lb.	sweet potatoes, peeled and cut in 2-inch pieces	3 lb.
2 cloves	garlic, halved	4 cloves
¼ cup	fat-free milk	½ cup
½ tsp.	salt	1 tsp.
12 oz.	uncooked ground turkey breast	24 oz.
½ cup	chopped onion	1 cup
1¼ cups	coarsely chopped zucchini	2½ cups
1 cup	chopped carrots	2 cups
½ cup	frozen whole kernel corn	1 cup
¼ cup	water	½ cup
1 8-oz. can	tomato sauce	2 8-oz. cans
2 Tbsp.	Worcestershire sauce	¼ cup
2 tsp.	snipped fresh sage	4 tsp.
⅛ tsp.	black pepper	¼ tsp.
	Fresh sage leaves (optional)	

CHAPTER 3

Meat

When supper calls for something substantial, satisfying, and absolutely sensational, you know where to turn—to the meat department. Take one of these recipes with you so you get everything needed to create a meaty masterpiece.

80

82

98

Wine-Glazed Steak

Simple sides—such as creamy garlic-mashed potatoes and steamed green beans—are all this steak needs.

1. Trim fat from steak; cut steak into two equal portions. In a large skillet heat oil over medium-high heat. Add steaks. Reduce heat to medium; cook for 10 to 13 minutes or until desired doneness (145°F for medium-rare or 160°F for medium), turning steaks occasionally. If steaks brown too quickly, reduce heat to medium-low. Transfer steaks to a serving platter; keep warm.

2. Add mushrooms, garlic, and crushed red pepper to skillet; cook and stir for 2 minutes. Remove skillet from heat. Carefully add wine. Return to heat. Boil gently, uncovered, for 3 to 5 minutes or until most of the liquid is evaporated. Add balsamic vinegar, soy sauce, and honey; return to simmering. Cook and stir about 2 minutes or until slightly thickened. Spoon over steaks.

***TIP:** If using the cranberry juice option, omit the honey.

PER SERVING *267 cal., 9 g total fat (2 g sat. fat), 48 mg chol., 336 mg sodium, 11 g carbo., 1 g fiber, 28 g pro.*

START TO FINISH: **30 MINUTES**

2 servings	ingredients	4 servings
1	boneless beef top sirloin steak, cut ½ to ¾ inch thick	2
2 tsp.	olive oil	4 tsp.
1 cup	sliced fresh mushrooms	2 cups
2 cloves	garlic, minced	4 cloves
⅛ tsp.	crushed red pepper	¼ tsp.
¼ cup	dry red wine or low-calorie cranberry juice*	½ cup
2 Tbsp.	balsamic vinegar	¼ cup
1 Tbsp.	reduced-sodium soy sauce	2 Tbsp.
1 tsp.	honey*	2 tsp.

Garlic Steaks with Nectarine Relish

If you feel compelled to make this dish when nectarines are not in season, use plump plums or juicy mangoes instead

1. Trim fat from steak. With the tip of a paring knife, make small slits in steak; insert half the garlic into slits. Wrap steak in plastic wrap; chill for 30 minutes. Sprinkle with salt and black pepper.

2. Meanwhile, for relish, in a large nonstick skillet cook onion and remaining garlic in hot oil over medium heat for 5 to 10 minutes or until onions are golden, stirring occasionally. Stir in vinegar and honey. Stir in nectarine and the snipped mint; heat through.

3. For a charcoal grill, place steak on grill rack directly over medium coals. Grill to desired doneness, turning once halfway through grilling. Allow 10 to 12 minutes for medium-rare (145°F) and 12 to 15 minutes for medium (160°F). (If using a gas grill, preheat grill. Reduce temperature to medium. Place steak on grill rack over heat; cover and grill as above.) Serve the steaks with relish. If desired, garnish with mint sprigs.

PER SERVING *274 cal., 13 g total fat (4 g sat. fat), 60 mg chol., 200 mg sodium, 15 g carbo., 2 g fiber, 24 g pro.*

PREP: 20 MINUTES
CHILL: 30 MINUTES
GRILL: 10 MINUTES

2 servings	ingredients	4 servings
1	boneless beef top loin steak, cut 1 inch thick	2
3 cloves	garlic, thinly sliced	6 cloves
⅛ tsp.	salt	¼ tsp.
⅛ tsp.	black pepper	¼ tsp.
1 medium	onion, coarsely chopped	2 medium
1 tsp.	olive oil	2 tsp.
1 Tbsp.	cider vinegar	2 Tbsp.
1 tsp.	honey	2 tsp.
1 small	nectarine, pitted and chopped	2 small
1 tsp.	snipped fresh mint	2 tsp.
	Fresh mint sprigs (optional)	

Fontina-Stuffed Tenderloin Steaks

If a hunt for fontina leaves you empty-handed, feel free to replace the nutty Italian cheese with easier-to-find Swiss or Jarlsburg cheese.

PREP: 25 MINUTES
ROAST: 12 MINUTES
OVEN: 400°F

2 servings	ingredients	4 servings
2 6-oz.	beef tenderloin steaks	4 6-oz.
½ cup	shredded fontina cheese	1 cup
1 Tbsp.	finely chopped oil-packed dried tomatoes	2 Tbsp.
1 tsp.	snipped fresh parsley	2 tsp.
½ tsp.	fresh thyme leaves	1 tsp.
1 small clove	garlic, minced	2 small cloves
1 thin slice	prosciutto, halved	2 thin slices
	Kosher salt and freshly ground black pepper	
1 Tbsp.	olive oil	2 Tbsp.
	Snipped fresh parsley (optional)	

1. Preheat oven to 400°F. Trim fat from steaks. Make a pocket in each steak by cutting horizontally from one side almost to the opposite side. Set aside.

2. For filling, in a small bowl combine cheese, dried tomatoes, 1 teaspoon parsley, thyme, and garlic. Divide filling on prosciutto halves; loosely roll up prosciutto around filling. Insert prosciutto bundles into pockets in steaks; secure with wooden toothpicks. Sprinkle steaks with salt and pepper.

3. In a medium skillet cook steaks in hot oil over medium-high heat until brown on both sides. Place steaks on a rack in a shallow baking pan. Roast for 12 to 15 minutes for medium-rare (145°F). Remove and discard toothpicks. If desired, sprinkle steaks with additional parsley.

FOR 4 SERVINGS: Prepare using method above, except in Step 2 use 2 teaspoons parsley.

PER SERVING 623 cal., 49 g total fat (19 g sat. fat), 145 mg chol., 688 mg sodium, 2 g carbo., 0 g fiber, 43 g pro.

Middle Eastern Beef Salad

Serve this fascinating steak salad with a side of flat bread so diners can use it to mop up every drop of the creamy mint dressing.

1. For the mint-yogurt dressing, in a bowl combine parsley, mint, garlic, olive oil, and honey. Stir in yogurt until well combined. Set aside.

2. Trim fat from steaks. Season steaks with salt and pepper. For a charcoal grill, place steaks on the grill rack directly over medium coals. Grill, uncovered, until desired doneness, turning once halfway through. Allow 10 to 12 minutes for medium-rare (145°F) or 12 to 15 minutes for medium (160°F). (For a gas grill, preheat grill. Reduce heat to medium. Place steaks on grill rack over heat. Cover and grill as above.)

3. Meanwhile, on 4 dinner plates arrange spinach, tomatoes, cucumber, and garbanzo beans.

4. Thinly slice the grilled steak and place on salad. Serve with mint-yogurt dressing.

FOR 8 SERVINGS: Prepare using method above, except in Step 3 use 8 dinner plates.

PER SERVING 282 cal., 9 g total fat (3 g sat. fat), 58 mg chol., 542 mg sodium, 25 g carbo., 6 g fiber, 27 g pro.

START TO FINISH: **30 MINUTES**

4 servings	ingredients	8 servings
¼ cup	snipped fresh parsley	½ cup
¼ cup	snipped fresh mint	½ cup
3 cloves	garlic, minced	6 cloves
1 tsp.	olive oil	2 tsp.
1 tsp.	honey	2 tsp.
6 Tbsp.	plain low-fat yogurt	¾ cup
12 oz.	beef tenderloin steaks, cut 1 inch thick	24 oz.
⅛ tsp.	salt	¼ tsp.
⅛ tsp.	black pepper	¼ tsp.
6 cups	packaged fresh baby spinach	12 cups
2 medium	yellow or red tomatoes, cut into wedges	4 medium
1 small	cucumber, coarsely chopped	2 small
1 15-oz. can	garbanzo beans (chickpeas), rinsed and drained	2 15-oz. cans

Easy Beef Burgundy

This is a perfect opportunity for introducing your family to healthful whole grain pasta. The technique of pairing something new—brown pasta—with something loved and familiar—beef—almost always works.

1. In a 3½- or 4-quart slow cooker combine onion soup, mushroom soup, and Burgundy. Stir in beef stew meat, mushrooms, and onion.

2. Cover and cook on low-heat setting for 8 to 10 hours or on high-heat setting for 4 to 5 hours. Serve over hot cooked pasta.

FOR 12 SERVINGS: Prepare using method above, except in Step 1 use a 5- or 6-quart slow cooker.

PER SERVING 354 cal., 9 g total fat (2 g sat. fat), 73 mg chol., 647 mg sodium, 33 g carbo., 2 g fiber, 30 g pro.

PREP: 15 MINUTES
COOK: 8 HOURS (LOW)

6 servings	ingredients	12 servings
1 10.75-oz. can	condensed cream of onion soup	2 10.75-oz. cans
1 10.75-oz. can	reduced-fat and reduced-sodium condensed cream of mushroom soup	2 10.75-oz. cans
¾ cup	Burgundy or other dry red wine	1½ cups
1½ lb.	beef stew meat, trimmed and cut into 1-inch cubes	3 lb.
8 oz.	fresh mushrooms, quartered	1 lb.
1 medium	onion, sliced	2 medium
6 oz.	whole wheat pasta or multigrain pasta, cooked and drained	12 oz.

Philly Steak Sandwiches

Bite into a bit of hoagie heaven.

PREP: **20 MINUTES**
BROIL: **17 MINUTES**

4 servings	ingredients	8 servings
1 12-oz.	boneless beef top sirloin steak, cut 1 inch thick	2 12-oz.
½ tsp.	garlic-pepper seasoning	1 tsp.
	Nonstick cooking spray	
2 medium	red and/or green sweet peppers, seeded and cut into thin strips	4 medium
1 large	onion, thinly sliced and separated into rings	2 large
4	whole wheat frankfurter buns, split	8
½ cup	shredded reduced-fat cheddar	1 cup

1. Preheat broiler. Trim fat from steak. Sprinkle steak with garlic-pepper seasoning. Place seasoned steak on the unheated rack of a broiler pan. Broil 3 to 4 inches from heat until desired doneness. Allow 15 to 17 minutes for medium-rare (145°F) or 20 to 22 minutes for medium (160°F).

2. Meanwhile, coat an unheated very large nonstick skillet with nonstick cooking spray. Preheat skillet over medium heat. Add sweet peppers and onion. Cover and cook for 5 minutes. Uncover and cook about 5 minutes more or just until tender, stirring occasionally.

3. Place split buns on a large baking sheet. Broil 4 to 5 inches from heat for 1 to 2 minutes or until lightly toasted. Remove bun tops from baking sheet; set aside. Slice steak into bite-size strips. Divide steak strips and sweet pepper mixture among bun bottoms. Sprinkle with cheese. Broil 4 to 5 inches from heat for 1 to 2 minutes or until cheese is melted. Top with bun tops.

PER SERVING *295 cal., 8 g total fat (3 g sat. fat), 46 mg chol., 416 mg sodium, 29 g carbo., 4 g fiber, 27 g pro.*

Roast Beef Panini

If you do not have a panini press or grill pan, simply make this sandwich as you would a grilled cheese sandwich—on a griddle or in a large skillet.

1. For the horseradish spread, in a bowl combine mayonnaise, horseradish, mustard, and caraway seeds. Set aside.

2. Lightly coat a panini press or griddle with nonstick cooking spray. Preheat over medium heat.

3. On one side of each bread slice spread horseradish spread. On half the slices place roast beef, watercress, cheese, and red onion. Top with remaining bread, spread sides down.

4. Cook sandwiches 3 minutes in the panini press or 5 minutes on a griddle, weighting with a skillet and turning once halfway through cooking time.

PER SERVING 333 cal., 11 g total fat (4 g sat. fat), 60 mg chol., 615 mg sodium, 32 g carbo., 4 g fiber, 24 g pro.

PREP: 25 MINUTES
COOK: 3 MINUTES

4 servings	ingredients	8 servings
2 Tbsp.	light mayonnaise	¼ cup
1 Tbsp.	prepared horseradish	2 Tbsp.
1 tsp.	Dijon mustard	2 tsp.
⅛ tsp.	caraway seeds	¼ tsp.
	Nonstick cooking spray	
8 slices	marble rye, rye, or pumpernickel bread	16 slices
8 oz.	cooked roast beef, sliced	1 lb.
1 cup	watercress or baby arugula	2 cups
2 slices	havarti cheese, halved	4 slices
¼ cup	thinly sliced red onion	½ cup

Beef Tenderloin with Tomato Jam

Tenderloin—beef's most luxurious cut—needs little in the way of seasoning or adornment. Just a little touch, like this garlicky sweet tomato jam, is perfectly elegant.

1. Preheat oven to 425°F. For tomato jam, in a 3-quart rectangular baking dish combine onion and garlic. Drizzle with the 2 tablespoons oil; toss gently to coat. Spread in a single layer. Roast, uncovered, for 15 minutes. Using a slotted spoon, remove garlic; set aside. Roast onion, uncovered, about 10 minutes more or until it starts to brown. Cool slightly. Coarsely chop onion and garlic. In a medium bowl stir together roasted onion and garlic, tomatoes, sugar, the ½ teaspoon salt, and the orange peel. Set aside.

2. Meanwhile, trim fat from meat. Brush meat with the 1 tablespoon oil; sprinkle with the 1 teaspoon salt and the pepper. Place meat on a rack in a shallow roasting pan. If desired, insert an oven-going meat thermometer into the center of the meat.

3. Roast, uncovered, for 35 to 40 minutes for medium-rare (135°F) or 45 to 50 minutes for medium (150°F). Remove tenderloin from oven. Cover with foil; let stand for 15 minutes before slicing. Temperature of meat after standing should be 145°F for medium-rare or 160°F for medium.

4. To serve, cut meat in ½-inch slices. Serve with tomato jam. If desired, garnish with thyme sprigs.

FOR 16 SERVINGS: Prepare using method above, except in Step 1 use two 3-quart rectangular baking dishes. Drizzle onion and garlic with 2 tablespoons oil. Use 1 teaspoon salt in the jam. In Step 2 brush each roast with 1 tablespoon oil and sprinkle with 2 teaspoons salt.

PER SERVING 308 cal., 17 g total fat (5 g sat. fat), 87 mg chol., 657 mg sodium, 7 g carbo., 0 g fiber, 30 g pro.

PREP: 35 MINUTES
ROAST: 35 MINUTES
STAND: 15 MINUTES
OVEN: 425°F

8 servings	ingredients	16 servings
1 medium	onion, cut in 1-inch wedges	2 medium
3 cloves	garlic, peeled	6 cloves
2 Tbsp.	olive oil	¼ cup
2 14.5-oz. cans	fire-roasted diced tomatoes, drained	4 14.5-oz. cans
½ tsp.	sugar	1 tsp.
½ tsp.	kosher salt	1 tsp.
½ tsp.	finely shredded orange peel	1 tsp.
1 2½-lb.	center-cut beef tenderloin roast	2 2½-lb.
1 Tbsp.	olive oil	2 Tbsp.
1 tsp.	kosher salt	2 tsp.
1 tsp.	freshly ground black pepper	2 tsp.
	Fresh thyme sprigs (optional)	

Beef and Three-Cheese Tortellini Salad

Remember this quick-as-a-wink salad the next time you have leftover beef roast in the fridge.

1. Cook tortellini according to package directions. Drain. Rinse with cold water; drain again.

2. In a large bowl combine tortellini, meat strips, cheese, broccoli, and squash. Drizzle salad dressing over beef mixture; toss gently to coat. Quick-chill in the freezer for 10 minutes or until ready to serve (or chill in the refrigerator for 4 to 24 hours).

3. To serve, line 4 salad plates with leaf lettuce. Divide salad among plates. If desired, garnish with cherry tomatoes.

PER SERVING *498 cal., 28 g total fat (12 g sat. fat), 97 mg chol., 822 mg sodium, 30 g carbo., 3 g fiber, 31 g pro.*

START TO FINISH: **30 MINUTES**

4 servings	ingredients	8 servings
2 cups	refrigerated or frozen cheese-filled tortellini	4 cups
8 oz.	cooked beef or cooked ham, cut in thin strips	1 lb.
1 cup	Colby jack or cheddar cheese cubes	2 cups
1 cup	broccoli florets	2 cups
1 small	yellow summer squash or zucchini, halved lengthwise and sliced	2 small
½ cup	Parmesan Italian salad dressing	1 cup
	Leaf lettuce	
	Cherry tomatoes, halved (optional)	

Baked Penne with Meat Sauce

Choose ribbed or smooth penne for baked dishes—either variety will soak up the sauce as it bakes.

1. Preheat oven to 350°F. Cook pasta according to package directions; drain well.

2. Meanwhile, in a large skillet cook ground beef and onion over medium heat until meat is browned, stirring to break up meat as it cooks. Drain off fat. Stir undrained tomatoes, tomato paste, wine, the water, sugar, dried oregano (if using), salt, and pepper into meat in skillet. Bring to boiling; reduce heat. Simmer, covered, for 10 minutes. Stir in pasta and olives. Spoon into a 3-quart rectangular baking dish.

3. Cover with foil. Bake about 20 minutes or until heated through. Sprinkle with mozzarella cheese. Bake, uncovered, about 5 minutes more or until cheese is melted.

FOR 12 SERVINGS: Prepare using method above, except in Step 2 use two 3-quart rectangular baking dishes.

PER SERVING *342 cal., 10 g total fat (4 g sat. fat), 51 mg chol., 465 mg sodium, 37 g carbo., 2 g fiber, 22 g pro.*

PREP: **30 MINUTES**
BAKE: **25 MINUTES**
OVEN: **350°F**

6 servings	ingredients	12 servings
8 oz.	dried penne pasta	1 lb.
1 lb.	lean ground beef	2 lb.
½ cup	chopped onion	1 cup
1 14.5-oz. can	diced tomatoes, undrained	2 14.5-oz. cans
½ of a 6-oz. can	Italian-style tomato paste	1 6-oz. can
⅓ cup	dry red wine or tomato juice	⅔ cup
⅓ cup	water	⅔ cup
½ tsp.	sugar	1 tsp.
½ tsp.	dried oregano, crushed	1 tsp.
¼ tsp.	salt	½ tsp.
¼ tsp.	black pepper	½ tsp.
¼ cup	sliced pitted ripe olives	½ cup
1 cup	shredded reduced-fat mozzarella cheese	2 cups

Cowboy Bowls

Hearty dishes like this are made for cold nights and hungry kids.

1. Heat mashed potatoes according to package directions.

2. Meanwhile, in a medium saucepan combine pork, undrained chili beans, corn, sweet pepper, and onion. Heat through.

3. Transfer mashed potatoes to shallow bowls. Top with pork mixture and sprinkle with cheese.

PER SERVING *600 cal., 21 g total fat (7 g sat. fat), 76 mg chol., 1,125 mg sodium, 74 g carbo., 8 g fiber, 31 g pro.*

START **TO FINISH: 20 MINUTES**

4 servings	ingredients	8 servings
1 24-oz. pkg.	refrigerated mashed potatoes	2 24-oz. pkgs.
1 17- to 18-oz. pkg.	refrigerated cooked shredded pork with barbecue sauce	2 17- to 18-oz. pkgs.
1 15- to 16-oz. can	chili beans in chili gravy	2 15- to 16-oz. cans
1 cup	frozen whole kernel corn	2 cups
½ cup	chopped red sweet pepper	1 cup
¼ cup	finely chopped onion	½ cup
½ cup	shredded cheddar cheese	1 cup

Mexican Beef Bake with Cilantro-Lime Cream

There is no middle ground with cilantro—people either love it or detest it. If your family is not fond of its piney, citrusy taste, feel free to substitute chopped chives or parsley in the creamy topper.

1. Preheat oven to 350°F. In a large saucepan cook pasta according to package directions; drain. Return pasta to hot saucepan; set aside.

2. Meanwhile, in a large skillet cook meat and garlic until meat is brown, stirring with a wooden spoon to break up meat as it cooks. Drain off fat.

3. Stir the cooked meat into pasta in saucepan. Stir in beans, tomatoes, picante sauce, oregano, cumin, and chili powder. Transfer mixture to an ungreased 1½- or 2-quart baking dish or casserole.

4. Bake, covered, about 30 minutes or until heated through. Sprinkle with cheese. Bake, uncovered, about 3 minutes more or until cheese is melted.

5. Meanwhile, for the cilantro-lime cream, in a small bowl stir together sour cream, 2 tablespoons of the green onions, cilantro, and lime peel. Serve beef with cilantro-lime cream, the remaining 1 tablespoon green onions, and, if desired, lime wedges.

FOR 12 SERVINGS: Prepare using method above, except in Step 3 use a 3-quart baking dish or casserole. In Step 5 use 4 tablespoons green onions for the cilantro-lime cream and pass the remaining 2 tablespoons.

PER SERVING 283 cal., 10 g total fat (4 g sat. fat), 45 mg chol., 520 mg sodium, 29 g carbo., 7 g fiber, 23 g pro.

PREP: 25 MINUTES
BAKE: 33 MINUTES
OVEN: 350°F

6 servings	ingredients	12 servings
4 oz.	packaged dried multigrain rotini macaroni	8 oz.
12 oz.	extra-lean ground beef	24 oz.
2 cloves	garlic, minced	4 cloves
1 15-oz. can	black beans or pinto beans, rinsed and drained	2 15-oz. cans
1 14.5-oz. can	no-salt-added diced tomatoes, undrained	2 14.5-oz. cans
¾ cup	bottled picante sauce or salsa	1½ cups
1 tsp.	dried oregano, crushed	2 tsp.
½ tsp.	ground cumin	1 tsp.
½ tsp.	chili powder	1 tsp.
½ cup	shredded reduced-fat Colby and Monterey Jack cheese	1 cup
⅓ cup	light sour cream	⅔ cup
3 Tbsp.	sliced green onions	6 Tbsp.
2 tsp.	coarsely snipped fresh cilantro	4 tsp.
½ tsp.	finely shredded lime peel	1 tsp.
	Lime wedges (optional)	

Southern Beefy Skillet

Grab a stack of Texas toast to sop up the extra spicy juices in this tomato-base skillet stew.

1. In a large skillet cook ground beef, celery, onion, and garlic over medium heat until browned. Drain off fat.

2. Add butter beans, undrained tomatoes, tomato sauce, sweet pepper, jalapeño, Worcestershire sauce, basil, oregano, hot pepper sauce, and black pepper. Bring to boiling. Reduce heat and simmer, uncovered, 10 to 15 minutes or until desired consistency.

PER SERVING *342 cal., 12 g total fat (5 g sat. fat), 74 mg chol., 499 mg sodium, 33 g carbo., 9 g fiber, 30 g pro.*

4 servings	ingredients	8 servings
1 lb.	lean ground beef	2 lb.
1 cup	chopped celery	2 cups
½ cup	chopped onion	1 cup
2 cloves	garlic, minced	4 cloves
1 15.5- to 16-oz. can	butter beans, rinsed and drained	2 15.5- oz. to 16-oz. cans
1 14.5-oz can	no-salt-added diced tomatoes	2 14.5-oz. cans
1 8-oz. can	no-salt-added tomato sauce	2 8-oz. cans
1 medium	green sweet pepper, cut in bite-size strips	2 medium
1	jalapeño, seeded and finely chopped (see tip, page 18)	2
2 tsp.	Worcestershire sauce	4 tsp.
1 tsp.	dried basil, crushed	2 tsp.
1 tsp.	dried oregano, crushed	2 tsp.
½ tsp.	bottled hot pepper sauce	1 tsp.
¼ tsp.	black pepper	½ tsp.

Chili-Style Macaroni and Cheese

Corn chips plus macaroni and cheese? Everyone will say, "Yes, please!"

1. Preheat oven to 350°F. Cook macaroni according to package directions; drain. Set aside.

2. For cheese sauce, in a medium saucepan cook onion in hot butter until tender. Stir in flour and pepper. Add milk all at once. Cook and stir over medium heat until slightly thickened and bubbly. Add cheeses, stirring until melted. Stir in cooked macaroni and chili beans in gravy. Transfer mixture to an ungreased 2-quart baking dish. Top with corn chips.

3. Bake, uncovered, for 25 to 30 minutes or until bubbly. Let stand for 10 minutes before serving. If desired, garnish with sliced green onion.

FOR 8 SERVINGS: Prepare using method above, except in Step 2 use a 3-quart baking dish.

PER SERVING *869 cal., 43 g total fat (24 g sat. fat), 112 mg chol., 1,358 mg sodium, 80 g carbo., 8 g fiber, 40 g pro.*

PREP: **25 MINUTES**
BAKE: **25 MINUTES**
STAND: **10 MINUTES**   OVEN: **350°F**

4 servings	ingredients	8 servings
8 oz.	packaged dried elbow macaroni	16 oz.
½ cup	chopped onion	1 cup
2 Tbsp.	butter or margarine	4 Tbsp.
2 Tbsp.	all-purpose flour	4 Tbsp.
⅛ tsp.	black pepper	¼ tsp.
2½ cups	milk	5 cups
1½ cups	shredded cheddar cheese	3 cups
1½ cups	shredded American cheese	3 cups
1 15-oz. can	chili beans in chili gravy	2 15-oz. cans
½ cup	corn chips, broken	1 cup
	Sliced green onion (optional)	

Tomato-Basil Burgers

Smeared with pesto mayo and topped with a slice of fresh mozzarella, this burger is hard to beat.

PREP: 15 MINUTES
GRILL: 11 MINUTES

4 servings	ingredients	8 servings
3 Tbsp.	mayonnaise	⅓ cup
2 Tbsp.	purchased basil pesto	¼ cup
	Salt and black pepper	
	Bottled hot pepper sauce	
1 lb.	lean ground beef	2 lb.
1 Tbsp.	finely chopped, drained, oil-packed dried tomatoes	2 Tbsp.
1 Tbsp.	snipped fresh basil	2 Tbsp.
½ tsp.	sea salt	1 tsp.
¼ tsp.	fresh cracked black pepper	½ tsp.
4 oz.	fresh mozzarella, sliced	8 oz.
4	kaiser or sourdough buns, split	8
1 cup	lightly packed fresh arugula or spinach	2 cups
⅓ cup	bottled roasted red sweet peppers, cut into strips	⅔ cup

1. For the pesto mayonnaise, in a small bowl stir together mayonnaise and pesto. Season to taste with salt, black pepper, and a few dashes hot pepper sauce.

2. In a medium bowl combine beef, tomatoes, basil, salt, and black pepper; mix lightly but thoroughly. Shape into four ½-inch-thick patties. Grill patties on the rack of an uncovered grill directly over medium heat for 10 to 13 minutes or until an instant-read thermometer inserted in side of patty registers 160°F, turning once.

3. During the last 1 to 2 minutes of grilling, top burgers with cheese and place buns, cut sides down, on grill rack to toast. Place arugula on bottom halves of toasted buns. Top with burgers, then roasted pepper strips. Spread pesto mayonnaise on top halves of toasted top halves of buns and place on peppers.

FOR 8 SERVINGS: Prepare using method above, except shape meat mixture into eight ½-inch-thick patties.

PER SERVING 328 cal., 5 g total fat (2 g sat. fat), 65 mg chol., 700 mg sodium, 33 g carbo., 2 g fiber, 35 g pro.

Lamb, Spinach, and Cauliflower Bake

In some areas of the country, good lamb is hard to find. If you live in one of those places, don't forgo this recipe—just use ground beef instead.

1. Preheat oven to 350°F. In a large skillet cook ground meat and onion until meat is browned and onion is tender, using a wooden spoon to break up meat as it cooks. Drain in a colander. Return meat mixture to skillet; add cauliflower. Cook and stir for 1 minute. Stir in garam masala and salt. Add spinach and cream cheese. Heat and stir just until cream cheese is melted. Spoon into an ungreased 2-quart square baking dish.

2. Bake, covered, for 20 to 25 minutes or until bubbly. If desired, sprinkle with peanuts and/or parsley. Serve with pita bread wedges or naan bread.

FOR 8 SERVINGS: Prepare using method above, except in Step 2 use a 3-quart baking dish.

PER SERVING 746 cal., 48 g total fat (23 g sat. fat), 147 mg chol., 944 mg sodium, 47 g carbo., 6 g fiber, 33 g pro.

PREP: 25 MINUTES
BAKE: 20 MINUTES
OVEN: 350°F

4 servings	ingredients	8 servings
1 lb.	lean ground lamb or ground beef	2 lb.
1 cup	chopped onion	2 cups
3 cups	cauliflower florets	6 cups
1 Tbsp.	garam masala	2 Tbsp.
½ tsp.	salt	1 tsp.
1 10-oz. pkg.	frozen chopped spinach, thawed and well drained	2 10-oz. pkgs.
1 8-oz. pkg.	cream cheese, cut up	2 8-oz. pkgs.
	Chopped peanuts (optional)	
	Chopped parsley (optional)	
	Pita bread wedges or naan bread	

Italian Pork with Mashed Sweet Potatoes

Remember Sunday suppers? Bring them back—with this pork roast as the centerpiece.

PREP: **20 MINUTES**
COOK: **8 HOURS (LOW)**

4 servings	ingredients	8 servings
1 tsp.	fennel seeds, crushed	2 tsp.
½ tsp.	dried oregano, crushed	1 tsp.
½ tsp.	garlic powder	1 tsp.
½ tsp.	paprika	1 tsp.
¼ tsp.	salt	½ tsp.
¼ tsp.	black pepper	½ tsp.
1 1½- to 2-lb.	boneless pork shoulder roast	1 3- to 4-lb.
1 lb.	sweet potatoes, peeled and cut into 1-inch pieces	2 lb.
1 cup	reduced-sodium chicken broth	2 cups

1. In a small bowl combine fennel seeds, oregano, garlic powder, paprika, salt, and pepper. Trim fat from roast. Sprinkle fennel seed mixture evenly over roast; rub in with your fingers. If necessary, cut roast to fit into a 3½- or 4-quart slow cooker. Set aside roast.

2. Place sweet potatoes in cooker. Add roast. Pour broth over all in cooker.

3. Cover and cook on low-heat setting for 8 to 10 hours or on high-heat setting for 4 to 5 hours.

4. Remove meat from cooker, reserving cooking liquid. Slice meat. Using a slotted spoon, transfer sweet potatoes to a medium bowl. Serve meat with sweet potatoes.

FOR 8 SERVINGS: Prepare using method above, except in Step 1 use a 5- or 6-quart slow cooker.

PER SERVING *341 cal., 10 g total fat (4 g sat. fat), 110 mg chol., 490 mg sodium, 24 g carbo., 4 g fiber, 36 g pro.*

Spiced Pork and Apples

Five-spice powder—a blend of cinnamon, anise, cloves, ginger, and fennel seed—is essential to many Asian-style dishes to which it provides a compellingly sweet, warm flavor.

1. Place pork chops in a resealable plastic bag set in a shallow dish; set aside. For marinade, in a small bowl combine peanut oil, honey, soy sauce, rice wine, sesame oil, five-spice powder, and ginger. Pour marinade over pork chops. Seal bag; turn to coat chops. Marinate in the refrigerator for 4 to 12 hours, turning occasionally.

2. Preheat oven to 425°F. Drain chops, reserving ¼ cup marinade. Arrange chops in an ungreased 3-quart oval baking dish. Arrange apples around chops. Drizzle apples with the reserved ¼ cup marinade. Sprinkle apples with cinnamon.

3. Bake, uncovered, for 10 minutes. Add green onions. Bake, uncovered, for 10 to 15 minutes more or until chops are cooked through (160°F) and apples are tender. Arrange chops and apples on a serving platter. Drizzle apples with honey.

FOR 8 SERVINGS: Prepare using method above, except in Step 2 arrange chops in 2 ungreased 3-quart oval baking dishes.

PER SERVING 539 cal., 28 g total fat (7 g sat. fat), 98 mg chol., 473 mg sodium, 42 g carbo., 3 g fiber, 31 g pro.

PREP: **25 MINUTES**   MARINATE: **4 HOURS**
BAKE: **20 MINUTES**   OVEN: **425°F**

4 servings	ingredients	8 servings
4	boneless pork chops, cut about ½ inch thick	8
¼ cup	peanut oil or vegetable oil	½ cup
¼ cup	honey or packed brown sugar	½ cup
¼ cup	reduced-sodium soy sauce	½ cup
2 Tbsp.	rice wine or sherry	4 Tbsp.
1 tsp.	toasted sesame oil	2 tsp.
1 tsp.	five-spice powder	2 tsp.
1 2-inch piece	fresh ginger, peeled and thinly sliced	2 2-inch pieces
2 large	baking apples (such as Cortland, Pippin, Rome Beauty, or Winesap), cored and cut in thick slices	4 large
¼ tsp.	ground cinnamon or five-spice powder	½ tsp.
4	green onions, diagonally sliced into 2-inch pieces	8
1 Tbsp.	honey	2 Tbsp.

Mushroom-Sauced Pork Chops

Tapioca? It's more than pudding! The starchy substance—extracted from yucca plants—is an excellent thickener that works just like cornstarch.

1. Trim fat from chops. In a large skillet heat oil over medium heat. Add chops; cook until browned, turning to brown evenly. Drain off fat. Place onion in a 3½- or 4-quart slow cooker. Add chops. Using a mortar and pestle, crush tapioca. In a medium bowl combine tapioca, mushroom soup, apple juice, Worcestershire sauce, thyme, and garlic powder; stir in mushrooms. Pour over chops in slow cooker.

2. Cover and cook on low-heat setting for 8 to 9 hours or on high-heat setting for 4 to to 4½ hours. If desired, garnish with thyme sprigs.

FOR 8 SERVINGS: Prepare using method above, except in Step 1 use a 5- or 6-quart slow cooker.

PER SERVING 330 cal., 10 g total fat (3 g sat. fat), 110 mg chol., 381 mg sodium, 17 g carbo., 1 g fiber, 39 g pro.

PREP: 20 MINUTES
COOK: 8 HOURS (LOW)

4 servings	ingredients	8 servings
4	pork loin chops, cut ¾ inch thick	8
1 Tbsp.	vegetable oil	2 Tbsp.
1 small	onion, thinly sliced	2 small
2 Tbsp.	quick-cooking tapioca	¼ cup
1 10.75-oz. can	reduced-fat and reduced-sodium condensed cream of mushroom soup	2 10.75-oz. cans
½ cup	apple juice or apple cider	1 cup
1 tsp.	Worcestershire sauce	2 tsp.
¾ tsp.	dried thyme, crushed	1½ tsp.
¼ tsp.	garlic powder	½ tsp.
1½ cups	sliced fresh mushrooms	3 cups
	Fresh thyme sprigs (optional)	

Pecan-Parmesan Pork with Port Sauce

There is no need to purchase a high-end Port for this dish. Inexpensive jug varieties do the trick perfectly.

1. Preheat oven to 425°F. Trim fat from tenderloins; set tenderloins aside. In a blender or food processor combine pecans, cheese, mustard, and Worcestershire sauce. Cover and blend or process until pecans are finely chopped. Press mixture onto all sides of the tenderloins to coat with a thin layer.

2. Place tenderloins, side by side, on a rack in a 3-quart baking dish. Roast, uncovered, for 25 to 35 minutes or until an instant-read thermometer inserted in center of tenderloin registers 155°F. Cover with foil; let stand for 15 minutes. Temperature of meat after standing should be 160°F.

3. Meanwhile, for sauce, in a medium saucepan stir together port, figs, and brown sugar. Bring to boiling; reduce heat. Simmer, uncovered, for 10 to 15 minutes or until mixture is reduced to about 1 cup. Cool slightly.

4. Transfer half the sauce to blender or processor. Cover and blend or process until nearly smooth. Pour sauce through a sieve over a bowl, pressing solids to release juices. Discard solids. Repeat with the remaining sauce. Return all the sauce to saucepan. Cook and stir over low heat just until heated through. To serve, slice meat. Serve with warm sauce.

FOR 8 SERVINGS: Prepare using method above, except in Step 3 reduce sauce to about 2½ cups.

PER SERVING *428 cal., 15 g total fat (3 g sat. fat), 78 mg chol., 253 mg sodium, 31 g carbo., 4 g fiber, 29 g pro.*

PREP: **25 MINUTES**
ROAST: **25 MINUTES**
STAND: **15 MINUTES**   OVEN: **425°F**

4 servings	ingredients	8 servings
1 1-lb.	pork tenderloins	2 1-lb.
½ cup	broken pecans	1 cup
⅓ cup	finely shredded Parmesan cheese	⅔ cup
4 tsp.	yellow mustard	2 Tbsp.
1 tsp.	Worcestershire sauce or soy sauce	2 tsp.
1 cup	port or dry Marsala	2 cup
½ cup	snipped dried Calimyrna or Mission figs	1 cup
1 Tbsp.	packed brown sugar	2 Tbsp.

Carnitas

Carnitas—or "little meats"—play many roles and are delicious eaten on their own, over rice, or placed in tamales, tacos, tortas, and burritos.

1. Sprinkle pork with salt and pepper. Place in a 3½- or 4-quart slow cooker.

2. To make a bouquet garni, cut a 6-inch square from a double thickness of 100%-cotton cheesecloth. Place peppercorns, cumin seeds, garlic, oregano, and bay leaves in center of cheesecloth square. Bring up corners of cheesecloth and tie with clean 100%-cotton kitchen string. Add to slow cooker. Add broth.

3. Cover and cook on low-heat setting for 10 to 12 hours or on high-heat setting for 4½ to 5 hours.

4. Using a slotted spoon, remove meat from slow cooker. Discard bouquet garni and cooking liquid. Using two forks, coarsely shred meat; discard any fat. Sprinkle meat with lime peel and lime juice; toss to mix. Serve on tortillas. Top with green onions. Top with sour cream and salsa, if desired.

FOR 12 SERVINGS: Prepare using method above, except in Step 1 use a 5- or 6-quart slow cooker.

PER SERVING 318 cal., 10 g total fat (3 g sat. fat), 90 mg chol., 377 mg sodium, 24 g carbo., 4 g fiber, 32 g pro.

PREP: **10 MINUTES**
COOK: **10 HOURS (LOW) or 4½ HOURS (HIGH)**

6 servings	ingredients	12 servings
1 2-lb.	boneless pork shoulder roast, cut into 2-inch pieces	2 2-lb.
¼ tsp.	salt	½ tsp.
¼ tsp.	black pepper	½ tsp.
1 Tbsp.	whole black peppercorns	2 Tbsp.
2 tsp.	cumin seeds	4 tsp.
4 cloves	garlic, minced	8 cloves
1 tsp.	dried oregano, crushed	2 tsp.
3	bay leaves	6
2 14-oz. cans	reduced-sodium chicken broth	4 14-oz. cans
2 tsp.	finely shredded lime peel	4 tsp.
2 Tbsp.	lime juice	¼ cup
12 6-inch	crisp corn tortillas	24 6-inch
2	green onions, thinly sliced	4
⅓ cup	light sour cream (optional)	⅔ cup
⅓ cup	purchased salsa (optional)	⅔ cup

Mexi-Pork Wraps

Mexican goes modern in this recipe, providing the burrito experience with a minimum of fat and calories.

1. In a large skillet heat oil over medium-high heat. Add pork and garlic to skillet; cook for 4 to 5 minutes or until pork is cooked through and juices run clear, stirring occasionally. Set aside.

2. In a medium bowl stir together corn, roasted red peppers, green onions, 2 tablespoons of the lime juice, the cumin, and cayenne pepper; set aside. In a small bowl stir together refried black beans and the remaining 1 tablespoon lime juice.

3. To assemble, spread 2 tablespoons of the black bean mixture in a 2-inch-wide strip down the center of each tortilla. Top with pork strips, corn mixture, romaine, and tomatoes. Fold bottom edge of each tortilla up and over the filling. Roll tortillas around filling. If desired, serve wraps with sour cream.

FOR 8 SERVINGS: Prepare using method above, except for the corn mixture in Step 2 use 4 tablespoons of the lime juice. Stir 2 tablespoons lime juice into the refried black beans.

PER SERVING 280 cal., 9 g total fat (2 g sat. fat), 39 mg chol., 419 mg sodium, 26 g carbo., 12 g fiber, 23 g pro.

START TO FINISH: **35 MINUTES**

4 servings	ingredients	8 servings
1 Tbsp.	olive oil	2 Tbsp.
8 oz.	lean boneless pork, cut into thin bite-size strips	1 lb.
1 clove	garlic, minced	2 cloves
½ cup	frozen whole kernel corn, thawed	1 cup
½ cup	chopped bottled roasted red sweet peppers	1 cup
¼ cup	sliced green onions	½ cup
3 Tbsp.	lime juice	6 Tbsp.
½ tsp.	ground cumin	1 tsp.
⅛ tsp.	cayenne pepper	¼ tsp.
½ cup	canned refried black beans or regular refried beans	1 cup
4 8-inch	whole grain tortillas	8 8-inch
½ cup	shredded romaine lettuce	1 cup
½ cup	chopped tomatoes	1 cup
	Light sour cream (optional)	

PREP: 25 MINUTES
BAKE: 35 MINUTES
STAND: 10 MINUTES
OVEN: 375°F

8 servings	ingredients	16 servings
12 oz.	dried campanelle or cellantani pasta	24 oz.
1 lb.	bulk Italian sausage	2 lb.
1 large	onion, cut in thin wedges	2 large
1 medium	yellow sweet pepper, cut in bite-size strips	2 medium
3 cloves	garlic, minced	6 cloves
1 24- to 28-oz. jar	marinara sauce	2 24- to 28-oz. jars
1 tsp.	fennel seeds, crushed	2 tsp.
1 15-oz. carton	ricotta cheese	2 15-oz. cartons
1	egg, lightly beaten	2
2 cups	shredded Italian blend cheeses	4 cups

Quick Lasagna Casserole

Campanelle is the lasagna noodle's "mini me."

1. Preheat oven to 375°F. Cook pasta according to package directions; drain.

2. In a large skillet cook sausage, onion, sweet pepper, and garlic until sausage is no longer pink; drain off fat. Transfer sausage mixture to a very large bowl. Stir in marinara sauce, fennel seeds, and cooked pasta.

3. Transfer the pasta mixture to eight 10-ounce ramekins or one 3-quart rectangular baking dish. In a medium bowl stir together ricotta cheese, egg, and 1 cup of the Italian blend cheeses. Spoon the ricotta cheese over the pasta mixture in large spoonfuls. Sprinkle the remaining shredded Italian blend cheeses over the top. Bake, covered, for 35 to 40 minutes or until heated through. Let stand 10 minutes before serving.

FOR 16 SERVINGS: Prepare using method above, except in Step 3 use sixteen 10-ounce ramekins or two 3-quart rectangular dishes. Stir 2 cups of the Italian blend cheeses into 2 eggs and the ricotta cheese

PER SERVING 636 cal., 35 g total fat (17 g sat. fat), 112 mg chol., 1,133 mg sodium, 47 g carbo., 5 g fiber, 34 g pro.

Cheesy Baked Penne and Sausage

It wouldn't be a bad idea to make two pans of this creamy mascarpone and Italian cheese sausage casserole. They'll be back for seconds.

1. Preheat oven to 350°F. Cook pasta according to package directions; drain. Meanwhile, in very large skillet cook sausage until browned; drain off fat. Stir in green onions; cook 1 minute. Add flour and mustard; gradually stir in milk and pepper. Cook and stir until slightly thickened and bubbly. Reduce heat; stir in mascarpone cheese until blended. Add remaining cheeses and pasta.

2. Transfer pasta mixture to a 2-quart rectangular baking dish. Bake, uncovered, for 25 to 30 minutes or until heated through.

FOR 12 SERVINGS: Prepare recipe using method above, except in Step 2 use a 3-quart rectangular baking dish.

PER SERVING 461 cal., 24 g total fat (14 g sat. fat), 74 mg chol., 687 mg sodium, 36 g carbo., 1 g fiber, 26 g pro.

PREP: 25 MINUTES
BAKE: 25 MINUTES
OVEN: 350°F

6 servings	ingredients	12 servings
8 oz.	dried penne pasta	1 lb.
8 oz.	bulk mild Italian sausage	1 lb.
⅓ cup	sliced green onions	⅔ cup
2 Tbsp.	all-purpose flour	¼ cup
2 Tbsp.	whole-grain mustard	¼ cup
1¼ cups	milk	2½ cups
¼ tsp.	pepper	½ tsp.
½ of a 8-oz. carton	mascarpone cheese	1 8-oz. carton
1 cup	shredded fontina cheese, shredded	2 cups
1 cup	shredded provolone cheese	2 cups

Sausage and Potato Lasagna

No knife needed! Prepackaged potato slices make this dish come together in a flash.

PREP: 30 MINUTES
BAKE: 35 MINUTES
STAND: 10 MINUTES
OVEN: 350°F

12 servings	ingredients	24 servings
1 20-oz. pkg.	refrigerated sliced potatoes	2 20-oz. pkgs.
½ cup	water	1 cup
1 lb.	bulk Italian sausage or bulk pork sausage	2 lb.
2 cups	sliced mushrooms	4 cups
½ cup	chopped onion	1 cup
2 cloves	garlic, minced	4 cloves
1 cup	milk	2 cups
1 Tbsp.	all-purpose flour	1 cup
½ tsp.	salt	1 tsp.
¼ tsp.	black pepper	½ tsp.
¼ tsp.	ground nutmeg	½ tsp.
1 15-oz. carton	ricotta cheese	2 15-oz. cartons
1 10-oz. pkg.	frozen chopped spinach, thawed and well drained	2 10-oz. pkgs.
½ cup	grated Parmesan cheese	1 cup
1	egg, slightly beaten	2
2 cups	shredded mozzarella cheese	4 cups

1. Preheat oven to 350°F. Grease a 3-quart rectangular baking dish; set aside. In a medium microwave-safe bowl combine potatoes and the water. Microwave, covered, on high about 5 minutes or until potatoes are almost tender, stirring once; drain and set aside.

2. In a very large skillet combine sausage, mushrooms, onion, and garlic. Cook over medium heat until sausage is brown. Drain off fat. In a medium bowl combine milk, flour, salt, pepper, and nutmeg. Stir milk mixture into sausage mixture in skillet. Cook and stir until thickened and bubbly; set aside.

3. In an extra-large bowl stir together ricotta cheese, spinach, Parmesan cheese, and egg. Layer half the sliced potatoes into the prepared dish. Spread half the ricotta cheese mixture and half the meat mixture on top. Sprinkle with half of the mozzarella cheese. Repeat with remaining potatoes, ricotta cheese mixture, and meat mixture.

4. Bake, covered, for 25 minutes. Uncover; sprinkle with remaining mozzarella cheese. Bake for 10 to 15 minutes more or until potatoes are tender and mixture is bubbly around edges. Let stand for 10 minutes before serving.

FOR 24 SERVINGS: Prepare using method above, except in Step 1 use two 3-quart rectangular baking dishes.

PER SERVING 462 cal., 27 g total fat (14 g sat. fat), 116 mg chol., 888 mg sodium, 22 g carbo., 2 g fiber, 28 g pro.

Kielbasa and Kraut Skillet

Kraut and sausage—sans the bun—is a super way to bring a summer grilling favorite inside for the winter.

1. In a large skillet cook kielbasa and onion just until onion is tender.

2. Stir in undrained sauerkraut, mustard, caraway seeds, salt, and pepper. Cook, covered, over medium heat about 10 minutes or until heated through.

PER SERVING *392 cal., 39 g total fat (16 g sat. fat), 50 mg chol., 1,755 mg sodium, 6 g carbo., 2 g fiber, 14 g pro.*

START TO FINISH: **25 MINUTES**

4 servings	ingredients	8 servings
1 lb.	cooked kielbasa, bias-sliced into 2-inch pieces	2 lb.
1 small	red onion, thinly sliced	2 small
1 15-oz. can	sauerkraut	2 15-oz. cans
1 Tbsp.	coarse-grain brown mustard	2 Tbsp.
¼ tsp.	caraway seeds	½ tsp.
¼ tsp.	salt	½ tsp.
¼ tsp.	black pepper	½ tsp.

CHAPTER 4

Seafood

Take a trip to the salty sea or paddle through clear inland waters with this collection of seafood suppers. They're guaranteed to make dinner the catch of the day.

116

120

125

Lemony Cod with Asparagus

Light and clean-tasting cod is known for its adaptability. This affordable whitefish takes to many flavor pairings, but lemon brings out its best.

1. Thaw fish, if frozen. Preheat broiler. Place breadsticks on the unheated rack of a broiler pan. Brush with 1 tablespoon of the melted butter and sprinkle with the garlic salt. Broil 4 inches from heat for 1 to 2 minutes or until golden brown, turning breadsticks once. Remove from pan and keep warm.

2. Meanwhile, rinse fish; pat dry with paper towels. Arrange fish and asparagus in a single layer on the same broiler pan rack.

3. In a small bowl stir together the remaining 1 tablespoon butter and the lemon juice. Drizzle butter mixture over fish and brush over asparagus. Sprinkle fish and asparagus with thyme and pepper.

4. Broil 4 inches from heat for 4 to 6 minutes or just until fish begins to flake easily when tested with a fork and asparagus is crisp-tender, turning asparagus once. Serve fish and asparagus with breadsticks and, if desired, lemon wedges.

FOR 8 SERVINGS: Prepare using method above, except in Step 3 use remaining 2 tablespoons butter and the lemon juice.

PER SERVING *293 cal., 8 g total fat (4 g sat. fat), 64 mg chol., 454 mg sodium, 29 g carbo., 3 g fiber, 27 g pro.*

START TO FINISH: **25 MINUTES**

4 servings	ingredients	8 servings
1 lb.	fresh or frozen skinless cod or flounder fillets, about ½ inch thick	2 lb.
4	soft breadsticks or 4-inch pieces of Italian or French bread	8
2 Tbsp.	butter or margarine, melted	¼ cup
¼ tsp.	garlic salt	½ tsp.
12 oz.	asparagus spears, trimmed	24 oz.
1 Tbsp.	lemon juice	2 Tbsp.
½ tsp.	dried thyme, crushed	1 tsp.
⅛ tsp.	black pepper	¼ tsp.
	Lemon wedges, halved crosswise (optional)	

Salmon with Roasted Vegetables

Go the extra mile and pass up farm-raised salmon for wild-caught salmon. Not only is it more environmentally sound, but it also contains more beneficial omega-3 fats and protein than its counterpart.

4 servings	ingredients	8 servings
4 4- to 5-oz.	fresh or frozen skinless salmon fillets, about 1 inch thick	8 4- to 5-oz.
	Nonstick cooking spray	
1 Tbsp.	snipped fresh dillweed	2 Tbsp.
½ tsp.	salt	1 tsp.
¼ tsp.	black pepper	½ tsp.
2 medium	zucchini and/or yellow summer squash, cut crosswise into ¼-inch-thick slices (about 2½ cups)	4 medium
1 cup	grape or cherry tomatoes, halved	2 cups
4	green onions, cut into 1-inch pieces	8
1 Tbsp.	Dijon mustard	2 Tbsp.

1. Preheat oven to 450°F. Thaw fish, if frozen. Rinse fish and pat dry with paper towels. Set aside. Line a 15×10×1-inch baking pan with foil; lightly coat foil with cooking spray. Set aside.

2. In a small bowl combine dillweed, salt, and pepper; set aside. In a large bowl combine zucchini and/or summer squash, tomatoes, and onions. Generously coat vegetables with cooking spray, tossing to coat evenly. Sprinkle with half the dillweed mixture, tossing to coat evenly.

3. Spoon vegetable mixture into one side of the prepared baking pan. Place fish in other side of pan. Stir mustard into remaining dillweed mixture. Spread mustard mixture evenly over fish. Measure thickness of fish in the thickest part of the fillets.

4. Bake, uncovered, for 4 to 6 minutes per ½-inch thickness of fish or until fish begins to flake when tested with a fork and zucchini is crisp-tender.

FOR 8 SERVINGS: Prepare using method above, except in Step 1 use two 3-quart rectangular baking pans.

PER SERVING *239 cal., 12 g total fat (3 g sat. fat), 66 mg chol., 463 mg sodium, 6 g carbo., 2 g fiber, 24 g pro.*

Salmon-and-Asparagus-Sauced Pasta

It's a spring thing. When Pacific salmon come into season, asparagus first pokes its funny-looking spears out of the ground. Join them up in this dish when both ingredients are at their flavorful best.

1. Snap off and discard woody bases from asparagus. If desired, scrape off scales. Bias-slice asparagus into 2-inch pieces.

2. In a large saucepan cook pasta according to package directions, except add asparagus the last 3 minutes of cooking. Drain; keep warm.

3. Meanwhile, for sauce, in a medium saucepan cook and stir sweet pepper and onion in hot butter over medium heat until tender. Stir in alfredo sauce, milk, and black pepper; heat through. Gently stir in salmon and tarragon; heat through. Add to pasta mixture and gently stir to combine.

PER SERVING 446 cal., 18 g total fat (11 g sat. fat), 54 mg chol., 910 mg sodium, 53 g carbo., 4 g fiber, 18 g pro.

START TO FINISH: **25 MINUTES**

4 servings	ingredients	8 servings
1 lb.	asparagus spears	2 lb.
2⅔ cups	dried cavatappi or penne pasta	5⅓ cups
1 small	red or yellow sweet pepper, cut into bite-size strips	2 small
½ cup	chopped onion	1 cup
1 Tbsp.	butter or margarine	2 Tbsp.
1 10-oz. container	refrigerated alfredo pasta sauce	2 10-oz. containers
¼ cup	milk	½ cup
⅛ tsp.	black pepper	¼ tsp.
3 oz.	lox-style smoked salmon, coarsely chopped	6 oz.
2 tsp.	snipped fresh tarragon	4 tsp.

Salmon-Dill Penne and Cheese

The salty crunch of crisp rye crackers accentuates the luxurious blend of smoked salmon and Havarti cheese with dill.

PREP: 25 MINUTES
BAKE: 30 MINUTES
OVEN: 350°F

4 servings	ingredients	8 servings
6 oz.	dried multigrain penne pasta	12 oz.
⅔ cups	whole milk	1¼ cup
8 oz.	Havarti cheese with dill, shredded	1 lb.
2 tsp.	all-purpose flour	1 Tbsp.
1 tsp.	finely shredded lemon peel	2 tsp.
⅛ tsp.	salt	¼ tsp.
4 oz.	smoked salmon, flaked, with skin and bones removed	8 oz.
½ cup	crushed crisp rye crackers	1 cup

1. Preheat oven to 350°F. Cook pasta according to package directions for minimum cooking time. Drain and return to pan. Stir in milk. In a medium bowl toss cheese with flour, lemon peel, and salt; stir into pasta mixture. Stir in salmon. Transfer to a 2-quart rectangular baking dish.

2. Cover and bake for 25 minutes; uncover. Gently stir and sprinkle with crushed crackers. Bake, uncovered, 5 to 10 minutes more or until heated through.

FOR 8 SERVINGS: Prepare using method above, except use a 3-quart baking dish.

PER SERVING *791 cal., 51 g total fat (10 g sat. fat), 160 mg chol., 1181 mg sodium, 43 g carbo., 4 g fiber, 43 g pro.*

Salmon Pasta Toss

Inexpensive ground Parmesan products—the kind that come in cylindrical packages—are fine in a pinch, but not for a fish as special as salmon. Splurge on the freshly ground stuff, and you'll be glad you did.

1. Combine pesto seasoning blend and olive oil Remove 1 tablespoon of the mixture and brush on salmon fillets. Broil salmon, 4 inches from heat, for 4 to 6 minutes per ½-inch thickness, turning once halfway through cooking, or until salmon flakes easily. Set aside.

2. Meanwhile, in a large pot cook fettuccine according to package directions. Drain well; return to pot. Stir in remaining pesto mixture, Alfredo sauce, undrained tomatoes, sweet peppers, half of the Parmesan cheese, and the milk. Heat through.

3. Break salmon into large chunks; gently fold into pasta mixture. Heat through. Transfer to a serving bowl. Sprinkle with the remaining Parmesan cheese.

FOR 12 SERVINGS: Prepare using method above, except in Step 1 use 2 tablespoons pesto mixture for the salmon fillets.

PER SERVING 561 cal., 24 g total fat (6 g sat. fat), 59 mg chol., 1,166 mg sodium, 56 g carbo., 3 g fiber, 29 g pro.

START TO FINISH: 25 MINUTES

6 servings	ingredients	12 servings
1 0.5-oz. envelope	pesto seasoning blend	2 0.5-oz. envelopes
3 Tbsp.	olive oil	6 Tbsp.
1 lb.	salmon fillets	2 lb.
12 oz.	dried fettuccine	24 oz.
1 16-oz. jar	dried tomato Alfredo sauce	2 16-oz. jars
1 14.5-oz. can	diced tomatoes with basil, oregano, and garlic, undrained	2 14.5-oz. cans
1 7-oz. jar	roasted red sweet peppers, drained and coarsely chopped	2 7-oz. jars
½ cup	finely shredded Parmesan cheese	1 cup
⅓ cup	milk	⅔ cup

Tuna and Hummus Wrap

Today's supermarkets are stocked with an interesting array of flavored hummus selections. Choose one you'd like to try—any of them are wonderful in this wrap.

START TO FINISH: **20 MINUTES**

4 servings	ingredients	8 servings
1 6-oz. can	very low sodium chunk white tuna (water pack), drained	2 6-oz. cans
1 small	cucumber, peeled, seeded, and finely chopped	1 medium
1 small	tomato, seeded and chopped	1 medium
2 Tbsp.	olive oil	¼ cup
1 Tbsp.	snipped fresh dill or 1 teaspoon dried dill, crushed	2 Tbsp.
¼ tsp.	black pepper	½ tsp.
⅓ cup	refrigerated cucumber-dill hummus	⅔ cup
4 8-inch	whole wheat tortillas	8 8-inch
4 cups	shredded packaged lettuce (such as hearts of romaine, European blend, or Mediterranean blend)	8 cups

1. In a medium bowl stir together tuna, cucumber, tomato, oil, dill, and pepper.

2. Spread hummus on one side of each tortilla. Toss tuna mixture with lettuce. Divide evenly among the tortillas. Roll up.

PER SERVING *280 cal., 11 g total fat (1 g sat. fat), 19 mg chol., 482 mg sodium, 32 g carbo., 4 g fiber, 16 g pro.*

Shrimp Pasta Diavolo

Diavolo is the Italian word for devil, and describes any dish that is made with spicy chiles.

1. Cook linguine according to package directions. Drain pasta and transfer to a very large bowl; set aside. Rinse shrimp; pat dry with paper towels.

2. Meanwhile, in a large skillet cook onion, garlic, and crushed red pepper in hot oil until tender. Stir in tomatoes. Bring to boiling; reduce heat. Simmer, uncovered, for 3 minutes. Add shrimp to skillet; cover and simmer for 3 minutes or until shrimp are opaque. Add shrimp mixture to pasta. Stir in basil and spinach. Top each serving with Parmesan cheese.

PER SERVING 412 cal., 13 g total fat (4 g sat. fat), 204 mg chol., 528 mg sodium, 44 g carbo., 4 g fiber, 30 g pro.

START TO FINISH: **20 MINUTES**

4 servings	ingredients	8 servings
1 9-oz. pkg.	refrigerated linguine	2 9-oz. pkgs.
12 oz.	medium fresh shrimp, peeled and deveined	24 oz.
1 medium	onion, cut into thin wedges	2 medium
3 cloves	garlic, minced	6 cloves
¼ tsp.	crushed red pepper	½ tsp.
2 Tbsp.	olive oil	¼ cup
1 14.5-oz. can	diced tomatoes, undrained	2 14.5-oz. cans
½ cup	torn fresh basil	1 cup
2 cups	fresh baby spinach	4 cups
½ cup	finely shredded Parmesan cheese	1 cup

Iceberg Wedges with Shrimp and Blue Cheese Dressing

This salad was the height of sophistication in the 1950s, when it was found in posh restaurants coast to coast. Bring it back to your table for a real retro feast.

1. Thaw shrimp, if frozen. Peel and devein shrimp, leaving tails intact if desired. Rinse shrimp; pat dry with paper towels. In a medium bowl combine shrimp, 2 tablespoons of the lemon juice, and ⅛ teaspoon of the black pepper. Toss to coat. Set aside.

2. For dressing, in a small bowl combine the remaining 1 tablespoon lemon juice, the remaining ⅛ teaspoon black pepper, the mayonnaise, and hot pepper sauce. Stir in blue cheese. Stir in enough of the milk to make desired consistency.

3. Coat an unheated grill pan with cooking spray. Preheat grill pan over medium-high heat. Thread shrimp onto six 10- to 12-inch-long skewers.* Place kabobs on grill pan. Cook for 3 to 5 minutes or until shrimp are opaque, turning once halfway through cooking. (If necessary, cook shrimp kabobs half at a time.)

4. Place 2 lettuce wedges on each of 6 serving plates. Top with shrimp, tomato, red onion, and bacon. Serve with dressing.

FOR 12 SERVINGS: Prepare using method above, except in Step 1 use a large bowl, 4 tablespoons of the lemon juice, and ¼ teaspoon of the black pepper. In Step 2 use remaining 2 tablespoons lemon juice and ¼ teaspoon black pepper. In Step 3 use 12 skewers.

PER SERVING 190 cal., 10 g total fat (2 g sat. fat), 129 mg chol., 360 mg sodium, 8 g carbo., 1 g fiber, 18 g pro.

* If using wooden skewers, soak them in water for 30 minutes before threading shrimp.

START TO FINISH: **35 MINUTES**

6 servings	ingredients	12 servings
1½ lb.	fresh or frozen large shrimp in shells	3 lb.
3 Tbsp.	lemon juice	6 Tbsp.
¼ tsp.	black pepper	½ tsp.
½ cup	light mayonnaise or salad dressing	¼ cup
¼ tsp.	bottled hot pepper sauce	½ tsp.
2 Tbsp.	crumbled blue cheese	¼ cup
3 Tbsp.	fat-free milk	6 Tbsp.
	Nonstick cooking spray	
1 large head	iceberg lettuce, cut into 12 wedges	2 large heads
1 large	tomato, chopped	2 large
⅓ cup	thinly sliced, quartered red onion	⅔ cup
2 slices	turkey bacon, cooked and crumbled	4 slices

Garlicky Peppers and Shrimp

To save time and eliminate the troublesome task of peeling and deveining shrimp, opt for those labeled "P & D," or peeled and deveined.

1. Cook pasta according to package directions; drain and return to pan. Toss with 2 tablespoons of the olive oil. Keep warm.

2. Meanwhile, in a very large skillet heat the remaining 2 tablespoons olive oil over medium-high heat. Stir in sweet peppers, onions, and garlic; stir-fry for 4 to 6 minutes or until crisp-tender. Add shrimp and cayenne pepper. Cook for 2 to 3 minutes or until shrimp are opaque, stirring occasionally.

3. Serve shrimp mixture over pasta. If desired, sprinkle with basil.

FOR 8 SERVINGS: Prepare using method above, except in Step 1 use ¼ cup of the olive oil. In Step 2 use the remaining ¼ cup olive oil.

PER SERVING *477 cal., 18 g total fat (3 g sat. fat), 229 mg chol., 256 mg sodium, 45 g carbo., 4 g fiber, 33 g pro.*

START TO FINISH: **20 MINUTES**

4 servings	ingredients	8 servings
1 9-oz. pkg.	refrigerated spinach or plain fettuccine	2 9-oz. pkgs.
4 Tbsp.	olive oil	½ cup
3 small	red, green, yellow, and/or orange sweet peppers, seeded and cut into thin strips	4 medium
2 medium	onions, cut into thin wedges	4 medium
4 cloves	garlic, thinly sliced	8 cloves
1 lb.	peeled and deveined medium shrimp	2 lb.
⅛ tsp.	cayenne pepper	¼ tsp.
1 cup	small fresh basil leaves (optional)	2 cups

Pasta with White Clam Sauce

This restaurant-style dish couldn't be easier—coming together in 30 minutes but tasting as if it took all day.

1. In a large saucepan cook pasta according to package directions. Drain; keep warm. Meanwhile, drain canned clams, reserving the juice from one of the cans (you should have about ½ cup). Add enough half-and-half to reserved clam juice to equal 2½ cups liquid. Set clams and clam juice mixture aside.

2. In a medium saucepan cook onion and garlic in hot butter over medium heat until tender but not brown. Stir in flour, salt, and pepper. Add clam juice mixture all at once. Cook and stir until thickened and bubbly. Cook and stir for 1 minute more. Stir in drained clams, oregano, parsley, and wine. Heat through. Serve over hot pasta. Sprinkle with Parmesan cheese.

FOR 8 SERVINGS: Prepare using method above, except in Step 1 you should have 1 cup clam juice and add enough half-and-half to equal 5 cups liquid.

PER SERVING *680 cal., 24 g total fat (14 g sat. fat), 125 mg chol., 430 mg sodium, 72 g carbo., 3 g fiber, 40 g pro.*

START TO FINISH: **30 MINUTES**

4 servings	ingredients	8 servings
10 oz.	dried linguine or fettuccine	20 oz.
2 6.5-oz. cans	chopped or minced clams	4 6.5-oz. cans
2 cups	half-and-half, light cream, or whole milk	4 cups
½ cup	chopped onion	1 cup
2 cloves	garlic, minced	4 cloves
2 Tbsp.	butter or margarine	¼ cup
¼ cup	all-purpose flour	½ cup
¼ tsp.	salt	½ tsp.
⅛ tsp.	black pepper	¼ tsp.
2 tsp.	snipped fresh oregano	4 tsp.
¼ cup	snipped fresh parsley	½ cup
¼ cup	dry white wine, nonalcoholic dry white wine, or chicken broth	½ cup
¼ cup	finely shredded or grated Parmesan cheese	½ cup

Mediterranean Scallops and Pasta

Resist the urge to use bottled lemon juice. It's worth the effort to squeeze fresh lemons. Not only does freshly squeezed juice provide a pure, zesty taste, but by using a fresh lemon you may also add grated lemon zest to the dish if you wish.

1. Thaw scallops, if frozen. Rinse scallops; pat dry with paper towels. Halve any large scallops. In a medium bowl combine oil, lemon juice, and Mediterranean seasoning; add scallops and toss to coat. Cover and chill for 15 minutes.

2. Meanwhile, in a 4-quart Dutch oven or saucepan cook pasta according to package directions. Drain well; return to hot Dutch oven. Add artichokes, tomatoes, and pesto to cooked pasta. Toss to coat. Keep warm.

3. In a large skillet bring scallop mixture to boiling over medium-high heat. Boil gently, uncovered, for 3 to 4 minutes or until scallops are opaque, turning scallops occasionally. Serve scallops over pasta mixture. Serve immediately.

FOR 8 SERVINGS: Prepare using method above, except in Step 2 use a 6-quart Dutch oven.

PER SERVING 537 cal., 22 g total fat (1 g sat. fat), 40 mg chol., 592 mg sodium, 54 g carbo., 2 g fiber, 29 g pro.

START TO FINISH: **30 MINUTES**

4 servings	ingredients	8 servings
1 lb.	fresh or frozen sea scallops	2 lb.
2 Tbsp.	olive oil	¼ cup
2 Tbsp.	lemon juice	¼ cup
2 tsp.	dried Mediterranean seasoning, crushed	4 tsp.
8 oz.	dried fettuccine	1 lb.
1 6-oz. jar	quartered marinated artichoke hearts, drained	2 6-oz. jars
¼ cup	oil-pack dried tomatoes, well drained and sliced	½ cup
¼ cup	purchased basil pesto	½ cup

Crab-Fennel Salad

Curried yogurt dressing drizzled across a freshly tossed combo of fresh melon, fruit, crabmeat, fennel, and greens makes a delicious, refreshing dinner for hot summer nights.

START TO FINISH: **20 MINUTES**

3 servings	ingredients	6 servings
⅓ cup	plain low-fat yogurt	⅔ cup
2 Tbsp.	mayonnaise or salad dressing	¼ cup
2 Tbsp.	milk	¼ cup
½ tsp.	curry powder	1 tsp.
2 cups	coarsely chopped fresh fruit, such as cantaloupe, strawberries, honeydew melon, and/or pineapple	4 cups
1 6- to 8-oz. pkg.	chunk-style imitation crabmeat or lobster	2 6- to 8-oz. pkgs.
¾ cup	sliced fennel	1½ cups
4 cups	torn mixed salad greens	8 cups

1. For dressing, in a small bowl stir together yogurt, mayonnaise, milk, and curry powder. If desired, thin dressing with additional milk. Set aside.

2. In a large bowl combine fresh fruit, crabmeat, and fennel; set aside. Divide salad greens among salad plates. Top with crabmeat mixture; drizzle with dressing.

PER SERVING *176 cal., 5 g total fat (1 g sat. fat), 16 mg chol., 601 mg sodium, 24 g carbo., 3 g fiber, 10 g pro.*

CHAPTER 5

Sides

It's time for those plain old peas and everyday taters to move over and make room on the plate. There are some new kids on the block, and these clever fruit, veggie, and rice concoctions are ready to move in—and make mealtime magic in the process.

135

140

149

Tropical Fruit Bowl

Papaya is one of nature's most nutritious fruits, full of antioxidants and digestive enzymes. If you're new to papaya, look for skin that is just starting to turn from shades of green to yellow, and a fruit that has slight give when pressed with the thumb.

1. Place pineapple, papaya, kiwifruits, and mangoes in an extra-large resealable plastic bag. Add honey and lime peel. Seal bag and turn gently to coat.

2. Chill fruit for at least 1 hour or up to 48 hours before serving.

3. Transfer fruit to a large serving bowl. Before serving, sprinkle fruit with toasted coconut and macadamia nuts.

* To toast whole or large pieces of nuts, spread them in a shallow pan. Toast them in a 350°F oven for 5 to 10 minutes, shaking the pan once or twice. Toast coconut in the same way, watching closely to avoid burning.

PER SERVING 142 cal., 5 g total fat (2 g sat. fat), 0 mg chol., 17 mg sodium, 26 g carbo., 3 g fiber, 2 g pro.

PREP: **30 MINUTES**
CHILL: **1 HOUR**

12 servings	ingredients	24 servings
1 medium	pineapple, peeled and cut into bite-size pieces	2 medium
1 large	papaya, halved, seeded, peeled, and cut into 1-inch cubes	2 large
4	kiwifruits, peeled and cut into bite-size pieces	8
2	mangoes, seeded, peeled, and cut into 1-inch cubes	4
¼ cup	honey	½ cup
1 tsp.	finely shredded lime peel	2 tsp.
½ cup	coconut, toasted*	1 cup
⅓ cup	coarsely chopped macadamia nuts, toasted*	⅔ cup

Maple Baked Stuffed Pears

The soft sweet texture of a freshly baked pear with a tart and crunchy combo filling of walnuts and cranberries dipped in a pool of maple syrup makes this an absolutely comforting side.

PREP: 20 MINUTES
BAKE: 40 MINUTES
OVEN: 350°F

4 servings	ingredients	8 servings
4 medium	firm pears with stems	8 medium
¼ cup	dried cranberries or dried tart red cherries	½ cup
3 Tbsp.	chopped walnuts, toasted	6 Tbsp.
1 Tbsp.	lemon juice	2 Tbsp.
2½ tsp.	sugar	2 Tbsp.
¼ cup	water	½ cup
¼ cup	pure maple syrup	½ cup

1. Preheat oven to 350°F. Cut a thin slice from the bottom of each pear so the pears stand up. Working through the bottom of each pear, use a melon baller to remove the core.

2. In a small bowl combine cranberries, walnuts, lemon juice, and sugar. Spoon cranberry mixture into the hollowed-out bottoms of pears. Stand pears in an ungreased 2-quart square baking dish. Add the water to baking dish. Pour maple syrup over and around pears. Sprinkle any remaining cranberry mixture into bottom of dish.

3. Bake, covered, for 20 minutes. Uncover; bake for 20 to 25 minutes more or until pears are tender, basting occasionally with cooking liquid.

4. To serve, spoon any remaining cooking liquid over pears. If desired, cut pears in half, topping with remaining filling from bottom of dish. Serve warm.

FOR 8 SERVINGS: Prepare using method above, except in Step 2 place pears in an ungreased 3-quart baking dish.

PER SERVING *219 cal., 4 g total fat (0 g sat. fat), 0 mg chol., 4 mg sodium, 49 g carbo., 6 g fiber, 1 g pro.*

Chunky Oven Applesauce

Whether you're young or old, homemade buttery brown sugar applesauce is always a special treat. Top it with berries for a quick snack or spoon it over grilled chops or roasted pork tenderloin.

PREP: 30 MINUTES
BAKE: 45 MINUTES
OVEN: 400°F

10 servings	ingredients	20 servings
6 medium	tart apples (such as McIntosh or Granny Smith), peeled, cored, and cut into ½- to 1-inch slices	12 medium
¼ cup	packed brown sugar	½ cup
2 Tbsp.	butter, cut up	¼ cup
2 Tbsp.	water	¼ cup
¼ tsp.	salt	½ tsp.
1	star anise	2
½ cup	fresh or frozen raspberries and/or blackberries, thawed	1 cup

1. Preheat oven to 400°F. Place apples in an ungreased 2-quart casserole or baking dish. Stir in brown sugar, butter, the water, salt, and star anise. Cover tightly with foil. Bake for 45 to 50 minutes or until apples are tender, gently stirring once or twice (cover with foil again after stirring).

2. Top with berries. Discard star anise. If desired, mash gently with a fork or carefully transfer mixture to a food processor; pulse with several on/off turns until smooth. Serve warm, at room temperature, or chilled. Cover and store leftovers in the refrigerator up to 3 days.

FOR 20 SERVINGS: Prepare using method above, except in Step 1 use an ungreased roasting pan.

PER SERVING 102 cal., 2 g total fat (1 g sat. fat), 6 mg chol., 77 mg sodium, 21 g carbo., 3 g fiber, 0 g pro.

Easy Coconut Rice

Nutty, aromatic jasmine rice is a must for this sensational side.

1. Preheat oven to 350°F. Place rice and peas in a lightly buttered 2-quart casserole or baking dish.

2. In a small saucepan combine the water, coconut milk, salt, and cinnamon; bring to boiling. Pour boiling liquid over rice. Bake, covered, about 30 minutes or until rice is tender. Let stand for 5 minutes. Stir before serving.

FOR 8 SERVINGS: Prepare using method above, except in Step 1 use a lightly buttered 3-quart casserole or baking dish.

PER SERVING *258 cal., 9 g total fat (8 g sat. fat), 0 mg chol., 318 mg sodium, 40 g carbo., 1 g fiber, 5 g pro.*

PREP: **10 MINUTES**
BAKE: **30 MINUTES**
STAND: **5 MINUTES**   OVEN: **350°F**

4 servings	ingredients	8 servings
1 cup	long grain rice (such as basmati or jasmine)	2 cups
½ cup	frozen peas, thawed	1 cup
1¼ cups	water	2½ cups
¾ cup	unsweetened coconut milk	1½ cups
½ tsp.	salt	1 tsp.
¼ tsp.	ground cinnamon	½ tsp.

Skillet Squash Cornbread

Two Southern side dishes—yellow squash casserole and cornbread—marry beautifully. For extra goodness, choose rustic-textured stoneground cornmeal.

1. Preheat oven to 400°F. In a large bowl stir together cornmeal, flour, sugar, baking powder, salt, and baking soda; set aside.

2. Coat a 9-inch cast-iron skillet or 9×1½-inch round metal baking pan with cooking spray. Place in hot oven for 2 minutes.

3. Meanwhile, in a medium bowl combine buttermilk and eggs. Add egg mixture all at once to flour mixture. Stir just until moistened. Gently stir in squash. Pour batter into hot skillet or pan. Bake for 25 to 30 minutes or until a wooden toothpick inserted near center comes out clean. Serve warm. If desired, serve with honey butter.

FOR 16 SERVINGS: Prepare using method above, except in Step 2 use two 9-inch cast iron skillets or 9×1½-inch round metal baking pans. In Step 3 evenly divide the batter between the two skillets or pans.

PER SERVING *150 cal., 3 g total fat (1 g sat. fat), 50 mg chol., 544 mg sodium, 27 g carbo., 2 g fiber, 6 g pro.*

PREP: **20 MINUTES**
BAKE: **25 MINUTES**
OVEN: **400°F**

8 servings	ingredients	16 servings
1 cup	yellow cornmeal	2 cups
¾ cup	whole wheat flour	1½ cups
1 Tbsp.	sugar	2 Tbsp.
2 tsp.	baking powder	4 tsp.
1 tsp.	salt	2 tsp.
½ tsp.	baking soda	1 tsp.
	Nonstick cooking spray	
1¼ cups	buttermilk	2½ cups
2	eggs, slightly beaten	4
1½ cups	finely shredded yellow summer squash or zucchini	3 cups
	Honey butter (optional)	

Rice Vermicelli Pilaf

Like the famous packaged "San Francisco treat," this homemade pilaf is quick and easy to make. Basil and bacon imbue it with enticing fresh flavors unavailable by the box.

PREP: 10 MINUTES
COOK: 20 MINUTES

4 servings	ingredients	8 servings
1 cup	long grain white rice	2 cups
½ cup	finely broken (½- to ¾-inch pieces) dried angel hair pasta	1 cup
⅓ cup	finely chopped onion	⅔ cup
3 Tbsp.	butter	6 Tbsp.
1 14-oz. can	chicken or beef broth	2 14-oz. cans
¼ cup	water	½ cup
¼ tsp.	salt	½ tsp.
¼ tsp.	black pepper	½ tsp.
	Snipped fresh basil, dill, and/or crumbled crisp-cooked bacon	

1. In a medium saucepan cook rice, angel hair pasta, and onion in hot butter over medium heat for 4 to 5 minutes or until pasta is lightly browned and onion is nearly tender. Carefully add broth, the water, salt, and pepper; bring to boiling. Reduce heat. Simmer, covered, for 15 to 20 minutes, or until the rice is tender and broth is absorbed.

2. Fluff pilaf with a fork. Sprinkle with basil and/or before serving.

FOR 8 SERVINGS: Prepare using method above, except in Step 1 use a large saucepan.

PER SERVING *336 cal., 9 g total fat (6 g sat. fat), 24 mg chol., 607 mg sodium, 55 g carbo., 1 g fiber, 7 g pro.*

Rosy Beet Risotto

If the rosy hue of this beet-blue cheese risotto is a little too colorful for your family, make it with yellow beets instead.

PREP: 15 MINUTES   ROAST: 1 HOUR 15 MINUTES
COOL: 30 MINUTES   COOK: 25 MINUTES
OVEN: 350°F

8 servings	ingredients	12 servings
12 oz.	beets	1 lb.
3 Tbsp.	olive oil	4 Tbsp.
½ cup	chopped red onion	¾ cup
1½ cups	Arborio or short-grain rice	2¼ cups
2 Tbsp.	snipped fresh basil or 1 teaspoon dried basil, crushed	3 Tbsp.
2 14-oz. cans	reduced-sodium chicken broth	3 14-oz. cans
½ cup	crumbled blue cheese	¾ cup
	Salt and freshly ground pepper	
	Fresh basil leaves	

1. Preheat oven to 350°F. Place beets in center of 18-inch square of heavy foil. Drizzle with 1 tablespoon olive oil. Fold together opposite edges of foil in double folds, allowing room for steam to build. Roast 1 hour and 15 minutes or until tender. Cool 30 minutes. Carefully open packet. Remove beets; gently transfer liquid to measuring cup; add water to equal ½ cup. Pour liquid in medium saucepan. Cut beets in wedges.

2. In a 3-quart saucepan cook onion in remaining oil over medium heat until tender; add rice. Cook and stir 5 minutes. Stir in dried basil, if using.

3. Meanwhile, add broth to beet liquid in saucepan. Bring to boiling. Reduce heat and simmer. Carefully stir 1 cup of hot broth into rice mixture. Cook, stirring frequently, over medium heat until liquid is absorbed. Then add ½ cup broth at a time, stirring frequently until broth is absorbed before adding more broth (about 22 minutes).

4. Stir in any remaining broth. Cook and stir just until rice is tender and creamy.

5. Add beets; heat through. Remove rice from heat; stir in half the cheese, snipped basil (if using), and salt and pepper to taste. Sprinkle remaining cheese and basil leaves.

FOR 12 SERVINGS: Prepare using method above, except in Step 2 use 1½ teaspoon dried basil, if using the dried herb option.

PER SERVING 185 cal., 7 g total fat (2 g sat. fat), 5 mg chol., 441 mg sodium, 26 g carbo., 1 g fiber, 5 g pro.

Corn-on-the-Cob Pudding

A great side for a brunch or holiday dinner, this spicy fresh corn and bread pudding is a trip down memory lane for those who grew up south of the Mason-Dixon line.

1. Lightly grease a 2-quart square baking dish; set aside. In a large skillet cook onion in hot oil over medium heat for 3 to 4 minutes or until tender, stirring occasionally. Stir in corn. Cook and stir for 2 minutes more. Cool slightly.

2. In a large bowl combine corn mixture, bread cubes, and jalapeños. In a medium bowl combine milk and egg. Pour milk mixture over bread mixture; stir gently to coat. Transfer mixture to the prepared baking dish. Cover and chill for 2 to 24 hours.

3. Preheat oven to 350°F. Bake, uncovered, about 45 minutes or until center is set and top is lightly browned. Let stand for 10 minutes before serving.

FOR 18 SERVINGS: Prepare using method above, except use a 3-quart baking dish. If using fresh eggs, use 6 eggs.

PER SERVING *136 cal., 2 g total fat (0 g sat. fat), 1 mg chol., 225 mg sodium, 22 g carbo., 2 g fiber, 7 g pro.*

PREP: **30 MINUTES**
CHILL: **2 HOURS**   BAKE: **45 MINUTES**
STAND: **10 MINUTES**   OVEN: **350°F**

12 servings	ingredients	18 servings
1 cup	finely chopped onion	1½ cups
1 Tbsp.	olive oil	4 tsp.
1½ cups	frozen whole kernel corn, thawed	2¼ cups
6 cups	1-inch cubes crusty country Italian bread	9 cups
2	fresh jalapeños, seeded and finely chopped (see tip, page 18)	3
2 cups	fat-free milk	3 cups
1 cup	refrigerated or frozen egg product, thawed, or 4 eggs, lightly beaten	1½ cups

Corn and Broccoli Bake

The crunchy, salty potato chip topping makes a great vehicle for getting veggies into little ones' mouths.

1. Preheat oven to 350°F. Place broccoli in a colander and run cold water over broccoli to separate. Drain well. In a medium bowl combine egg, corn, crushed crackers, and pepper. Stir in broccoli.

2. Divide broccoli mixture among 6 ungreased 6-ounce baking dishes. Top with cheese. In a small bowl combine crushed potato chips and melted butter; sprinkle over broccoli mixture.

3. Place baking dishes in a shallow baking pan. Bake, uncovered, about 35 minutes or until heated through.

FOR 12 SERVINGS: Prepare using method above, except in Step 2 use 12 ungreased 6-ounce baking dishes.

PER SERVING *244 cal., 14 g total fat (6 g sat. fat), 55 mg chol., 528 mg sodium, 25 g carbo., 2 g fiber, 7 g pro.*

PREP: **20 MINUTES**
BAKE: **35 MINUTES**
OVEN: **350°F**

6 servings	ingredients	12 servings
1 10-oz. pkg.	frozen cut broccoli	2 10-oz. pkgs.
1	egg, lightly beaten	2
1 14.75-oz. can	cream-style corn	2 14.75-oz. cans
⅔ cup	crushed rich round crackers	1⅓ cups
⅛ tsp.	seasoned pepper	¼ tsp.
3 slices	process American cheese food (.75 ounce each), halved	6 slices
1 cup	crushed potato chips	2 cups
2 Tbsp.	butter, melted	4 Tbsp.

Skillet Corn

Serve this edamame, corn, and tomato and pepper Texas caviar spooned over a tender, juicy grilled steak or served in a crispy flour tortilla shell with a taco salad.

1. In a large skillet cook bacon over medium heat until crisp. Remove bacon and drain on paper towels, reserving 2 tablespoons of the drippings in skillet. Discard the remaining drippings. Crumble bacon; set aside. Add corn and soybeans to the reserved drippings. Cook and stir for 3 to 4 minutes or just until vegetables are crisp-tender.

2. In a large bowl stir together crumbled bacon, corn and soybeans, tomatoes, red onion, cilantro, and jalapeño pepper.

3. For dressing, in a screw-top jar combine oil, lime peel, lime juice, garlic, cumin, salt, and chili powder. Cover and shake well. Pour dressing over corn mixture; toss gently to coat.

PER ½-CUP SERVING *182 cal., 11 g total fat (3 g sat. fat), 9 mg chol., 160 mg sodium, 17 g carbo., 3 g fiber, 7 g pro.*

START TO FINISH: **35 MINUTES**

6 servings	ingredients	12 servings
4 slices	bacon	8 slices
2 cups	fresh or frozen corn kernels	4 cups
1 cup	frozen shelled sweet soybeans (edamame)	2 cups
1 cup	grape or cherry tomatoes, halved	2 cups
½ small	red onion, thinly sliced	1 small
2 Tbsp.	snipped fresh cilantro	¼ cup
1 small	fresh jalapeño, seeded and finely chopped (see tip, page 18)	2 small
1 Tbsp.	olive oil	2 Tbsp.
½ tsp.	finely shredded lime peel	1 tsp.
1 Tbsp.	lime juice	2 Tbsp.
2 cloves	garlic, minced	4 cloves
¼ tsp.	ground cumin	½ tsp.
⅛ tsp.	salt	¼ tsp.
⅛ tsp.	chili powder	¼ tsp.

Mashed Sweet Potatoes with White Cheddar

Make substituting sweet potatoes for white potatoes a weekly habit. The tubers' beautiful color brighten plates and their color tells you that they are nutritional powerhouses.

1. Preheat oven to 425°F. Scrub potatoes and prick with fork; place on foil-lined baking sheet. Bake 40 minutes or until tender. Reduce oven temperature to 325°F.

2. When potatoes are cool enough to handle, scrape pulp from skin. Transfer to bowl. Mash with 2 tablespoons of the butter and ¾ teaspoon of the salt. Stir in cheese, bourbon, cream and 2 tablespoons of the brown sugar. Transfer to buttered 1½-quart casserole. Cover; bake 30 minutes or until heated through.

3. Meanwhile, in microwave-safe 2-quart casserole combine remaining butter, brown sugar, and salt; add onion. Microwave, uncovered, on high for 3 to 4 minutes or until onion is crisp-tender; add apples. Cover and cook 2 minutes more or until apples are tender. Stir in thyme and pepper. Serve with sweet potatoes.

FOR 12 SERVINGS: Prepare using method above, except in Step 2 mash potatoes with 3 tablespoons of the butter and ¾ teaspoon of the salt. Stir in cheese, bourbon, cream, and 3 tablespoons of the brown sugar. Transfer to a buttered 2-quart casserole. In Step 3 use a 3-quart microwave-safe casserole.

PER SERVING *293 cal., 12 g total fat (8 g sat. fat), 37 mg chol., 421 mg sodium, 38 g carbo., 5 g fiber, 5 g pro.*

PREP: 40 MINUTES
BAKE: 1 HOUR 10 MINUTES
COOK: 5 MINUTES   OVEN: 425°F/325°F

8 servings	ingredients	12 servings
3 lb.	sweet potatoes	4½ lb.
¼ cup	butter	6 Tbsp.
1 tsp.	kosher salt or salt	1½ tsp.
3 oz.	aged white cheddar cheese, shredded	5 oz.
¼ cup	bourbon or orange juice	6 Tbsp.
¼ cup	whipping cream	6 Tbsp.
¼ cup	packed dark brown sugar	6 Tbsp.
1 large	red onion, cut into thin wedges	2 medium
2 medium	red apples, cored and cut into wedges	3 medium
2 tsp.	snipped fresh thyme	3 tsp.
¼ tsp.	black pepper	¼ tsp.

Tuscan Cheese-Potato Bake

With a dusting of crispy bread crumbs and a hint of Italian cheese and herb flavor, these skin-on mashed potatoes are a great platform for a beef tenderloin steak or crunchy fried chicken.

PREP: 30 MINUTES
BAKE: 20 MINUTES
OVEN: 400°F

8 servings	ingredients	16 servings
2 lb.	red potatoes	4 lb.
¼ cup	butter	½ cup
3 cloves	garlic, minced	6 cloves
1½ tsp.	snipped fresh thyme*	3 tsp.
1 cup	buttermilk	2 cups
½ tsp.	salt	1 tsp.
¼ tsp.	black pepper	½ tsp.
1 cup	shredded fontina cheese	2 cups
1 cup	finely shredded Parmesan cheese	2 cups
⅓ cup	crumbled blue cheese	⅔ cup
½ cup	panko (Japanese-style bread crumbs)	1 cup
¼ tsp.	dried Italian seasoning, crushed	½ tsp.
1 Tbsp.	olive oil	2 Tbsp.
	Snipped fresh parsley (optional)	

1. Preheat oven to 400°F. Lightly grease a 2-quart square baking dish; set aside. Scrub potatoes; cut in 1-inch pieces. In a large saucepan cook potatoes in enough boiling, lightly salted water to cover for 12 to 15 minutes or until tender; drain.

2. In a 12-inch skillet melt butter over medium heat. Add garlic and thyme; cook and stir for 1 minute. Add potatoes; coarsely mash with a potato masher. Stir in buttermilk, salt, and pepper. Fold in fontina cheese, ½ cup of the Parmesan cheese, and the blue cheese. Transfer mixture to the prepared baking dish, spreading evenly.

3. In a small bowl combine the remaining ½ cup Parmesan cheese, panko, and Italian seasoning. Drizzle with oil; toss gently to coat. Sprinkle evenly over potato mixture.

4. Bake, uncovered, about 20 minutes or until mixture is bubbly and top is golden brown. If desired, sprinkle with parsley.

FOR 16 SERVINGS: Prepare using method above, except in Step 1 use a 3-quart rectangular baking dish. In Step 2 and in Step 3 use 1 cup finely shredded Parmesan cheese. Increase bake time to 20 to 30 minutes.

* Instead of the fresh snipped thyme you may use ½ teaspoon dried thyme, crushed, for 8 servings and 1 teaspoon for 16 servings.

PER SERVING 304 cal., 18 g total fat (10 g sat. fat), 47 mg chol., 653 mg sodium, 23 g carbo., 2 g fiber, 14 g pro.

Creamy Brussels Sprouts with Peppered Bacon

If you're in a pinch and don't have peppered bacon on hand, try a little pancetta or thick-cut bacon as a stand-in, then grind a generous dose of black pepper into the mix.

1. In a large skillet cook bacon over medium heat until browned and crisp. Drain on paper towels, reserving 2 tablespoons drippings in skillet.

2. Add Brussels sprouts to drippings in skillet. Cook on medium heat 4 minutes, stirring occasionally. Add broth, salt, and pepper. Heat to boiling. Reduce heat. Simmer, covered, for 5 minutes. Uncover; cook 2 to 4 minutes more or until liquid is almost evaporated. Add cream. Cook 4 minutes more or until thickened.

3. Transfer sprouts to serving dish. Sprinkle with crumbled bacon and cracked pepper.

PER SERVING *174 cal., 14 g total fat (7 g sat. fat), 38 mg chol., 305 mg sodium, 10 g carbo., 4 g fiber, 6 g pro.*

PREP: 20 MINUTES
COOK: 15 MINUTES

8 servings	ingredients	12 servings
4 slices	peppered bacon	6 slices
2 lb.	Brussels sprouts, trimmed and halved through stem end	3 lb.
¾ cup	reduced-sodium chicken broth	1 cup
½ tsp.	kosher salt	¾ tsp.
¼ tsp.	freshly ground black pepper	¼ tsp.
¾ cup	whipping cream	1 cup
	Cracked black pepper	

Boston Baked Beans with Pancetta

Bring these baked beans and bacon to your next potluck party or serve them to the family on burger and hot dog night.

6 servings	ingredients	12 servings
8 oz.	Great Northern beans or dried navy beans	1 lb.
3 oz.	pancetta or bacon, chopped	6 oz.
½ cup	chopped onion	1 cup
2 Tbsp.	packed brown sugar	¼ cup
2 Tbsp.	pure maple syrup	⅓ cup
2 Tbsp.	Worcestershire sauce	¼ cup
¾ tsp.	dry mustard	1½ tsp.
¼ tsp.	salt	½ tsp.
⅛ tsp.	black pepper	¼ tsp.
2 oz.	pancetta or bacon, chopped, crisp-cooked, and drained (optional)	4 oz.

1. Rinse beans. In a 2½- or 3-quart ovenproof Dutch oven combine beans and 4 cups water. Bring to boiling; reduce heat. Simmer, uncovered, for 2 minutes. Remove from heat. Cover and let stand for 1 hour. (Or combine beans and 8 cups water in Dutch oven. Cover and let soak in a cool place overnight.) Drain and rinse beans.

2. Return beans to Dutch oven. Stir in 8 cups fresh water. Bring to boiling; reduce heat. Cover and simmer for 1 to 1¼ hours or until beans are tender, stirring occasionally. Drain beans, reserving liquid.

3. Preheat oven to 300°F. In the same Dutch oven cook the 3 ounces pancetta and the onion over medium heat until pancetta is slightly crisp and onion is tender, stirring occasionally. Add brown sugar; cook and stir until sugar is dissolved. Stir in maple syrup, Worcestershire sauce, dry mustard, salt, and pepper. Stir in drained beans and ¾ cup of the reserved bean liquid.

4. Bake, covered, for 1 hour. Uncover and bake for 30 to 45 minutes more or until desired consistency, stirring occasionally. Beans will thicken slightly as they cool. If necessary, stir in additional reserved bean liquid. (Or spoon bean mixture into twelve 8-ounce ramekins. Bake, covered, for 20 minutes. Uncover and bake 10 minutes more.) If desired, sprinkle with the 2 ounces cooked pancetta.

FOR 12 SERVINGS: Prepare using method above, except in Step 1 use a 4- or 5-quart ovenproof Dutch oven and 8 cups water. In Step 3 use 6 ounces pancetta and stir in 1½ cups of the reserved bean liquid. If making individual servings, in Step 4 use twelve 8-ounce ramekins and top with 4 ounces of the pancetta.

PER SERVING 275 cal., 6 g total fat (2 g sat. fat), 12 mg chol., 507 mg sodium, 44 g carbo., 7 g fiber, 12 g pro.

Broccoli Rabe with Garlic

A close cousin to broccoli, rabe's thin broccoli-like florets are a staple in southern Italy. Sautéed with garlic, this tender veggie goes well with several entrées, including pastas, steaks, and poultry.

1. If using broccoli raab, remove large leaves and, if necessary, cut stems to 6- to 8-inch-long pieces. In a 6- to 8-quart Dutch oven cook broccoli raab or broccoli, half at a time if necessary, in a large amount of boiling water for 3 minutes if using broccoli raab or 6 minutes if using broccoli florets. Drain well; gently squeeze broccoli raab if necessary to get it really dry.

2. In the same Dutch oven heat oil on medium heat. Add garlic; cook and stir for 30 seconds. Carefully add drained broccoli raab or broccoli florets (the oil will spatter if the vegetables are not drained well); cook and stir for 1 minute. Add broth and cook, uncovered, until all of the broth has evaporated, stirring frequently. Stir in pepper and salt. Serve immediately.

* Instead of the broccoli rabe you may use 5 cups broccoli florets for 8 servings or 7 cups for 12 servings.

PER SERVING *48 cal., 3 g total fat (0 g sat. fat), 0 mg chol., 98 mg sodium, 4 g carbo., 3 g fiber, 4 g pro.*

START TO FINISH: **20 MINUTES**

8 servings	ingredients	12 servings
2 lb.	broccoli raab*	3 lb.
4 tsp.	olive oil	2 Tbsp.
4 cloves	garlic, minced	6 cloves
3 Tbsp.	reduced-sodium chicken broth	¼ cup
¼ tsp.	black pepper	¼ tsp.
¼ tsp.	salt	¼ tsp.

Fennel Slaw

Serve this crispy fennel slaw next to lasagna or other rich and cheesy pasta dishes. Cool, anise-flavor fennel makes a nice light accompaniment to southern Italian foods.

1. Trim any brown spots from fennel and cut a thin slice off base of bulbs. Discard green stems. Cut fennel in half lengthwise, then cut crosswise into thin slices.

2. Combine fennel, olives, and parsley in large bowl. In a small bowl whisk together oil, vinegar, garlic, salt, and crushed red pepper. Add to fennel mixture; toss to coat. Cover and refrigerate 1 to 24 hours.

PER SERVING *128 cal., 12 g total fat (2 g sat. fat), 0 mg chol., 391 mg sodium, 6 g carbo., 3 g fiber, 1 g pro.*

PREP: 25 MINUTES
CHILL: 1 HOUR

8 servings	ingredients	16 servings
2 medium	fennel bulbs	4 medium
1 cup	large green olives, pitted and sliced	2 cups
⅓ cup	chopped fresh parsley	⅔ cup
⅓ cup	olive oil	⅔ cup
3 Tbsp.	red wine vinegar	6 Tbsp.
4 cloves	garlic, minced	8 cloves
¼ tsp.	salt	½ tsp.
¼ tsp.	crushed red pepper	½ tsp.

Sicilian Escarole Salad

Escarole is a close cousin of bitter-leaved endive, but the ruffled, loose leaves of escarole are quite mild and refreshing.

1. For dressing, in a screw-top jar combine olive oil, vinegar, anchovy, garlic, basil, oregano, salt, red pepper, and black pepper. Cover; shake well.

2. In a very large salad bowl combine escarole, lettuce, cucumber, olives, and onion. Add desired stir-ins. Just before serving, pour dressing over salad and toss well.

PER SERVING (WITHOUT STIR-INS) *93 cal., 8 g total fat (1 g sat. fat), 4 mg chol., 319 mg sodium, 4 g carbo., 2 g fiber, 2 g pro.*

PREP: **20 MINUTES**

6 servings	ingredients	12 servings
3 Tbsp.	olive oil	6 Tbsp.
1 Tbsp.	white wine vinegar	2 Tbsp.
½ of a 2-oz. can	anchovy filets, drained and chopped	1 2-oz. can
1 clove	garlic, minced	2 cloves
¼ tsp.	dried basil	½ tsp.
¼ tsp.	dried oregano, crushed	½ tsp.
⅛ tsp.	salt	¼ tsp.
⅛ tsp.	crushed red pepper	¼ tsp.
Dash	black pepper	⅛ tsp.
3 cups	torn escarole	6 cups
3 cups	torn leaf lettuce	6 cups
1 small	English cucumber, quartered lengthwise and sliced into ½-inch chunks	1 medium
½ cup	pitted ripe olives or oil-cured black olives, chopped	1 cup
½ cup	thinly sliced red onion	1 cup
1½ cups	assorted stir-ins such as chopped roasted red sweet peppers; drained and rinsed cannellini beans; drained and flaked tuna (oil packed); tomato slices; chopped salami; cubed Asiago cheese	3 cups

CHAPTER 6

Desserts

Everyone loves a little sweet talk—especially at the end of a homemade meal. And the super-easy bars, cakes, pies, and puddings on these pages know just what to say.

167

183

184

Honey-Glazed Buttermilk Oatmeal Coffee Cake

Buttermilk is a miraculous ingredient, and you'll love tasting its rich tangy goodness in this coffee cake. Dairy buttermilk is best, but if you don't have any on hand, feel free to make your own by mixing a tablespoon of vinegar to a cup of milk and letting it stand for 5 minutes.

1. Preheat oven to 375°F. Grease a 9×9×2-inch baking pan. In a small bowl combine honey, ⅓ cup melted butter, corn syrup, lemon peel, and lemon juice. Stir in ½ cup chopped pecans. Pour into prepared pan; set aside.

2. For cake, in a blender or food processor, blend or process oats until finely ground. Transfer to a large bowl. Stir in flour, brown sugar, ½ cup pecans, baking powder, baking soda, and salt. Make a well in the center of the dry ingredients. In a medium bowl combine buttermilk, eggs, ¼ cup melted butter, and vanilla. Add the milk mixture all at once to the flour mixture. Stir just until moistened (batter should be lumpy).

3. Spoon batter evenly over honey mixture. Bake for 25 minutes or until a wooden toothpick inserted in center comes out clean. Remove from oven and immediately invert cake onto a serving plate. Cool about 10 minutes. Serve warm. If desired, drizzled with additional honey.

FOR 18 SERVINGS: prepare using method above, except in Step 1 use two 9×9×2-inch baking pans. Combine honey with ⅔ cup melted butter; stir in 1 cup of the pecans. in Step 2, use ½ cup butter. Divide honey mixture evenly among the two prepared pans. In Step 3 divide batter evenly over honey mixture.

PER SERVING 450 cal., 23 g total fat (9 g sat. fat), 79 mg chol., 357 mg sodium, 58 g carbo., 3 g fiber, 6 g pro.

PREP: 30 MINUTES
BAKE: 25 MINUTES
OVEN: 375°F

9 servings	ingredients	18 servings
½ cup	honey	1 cup
⅓ cup	butter, melted	⅔ cup
2 Tbsp.	light-color corn syrup	¼ cup
2 tsp.	finely shredded lemon peel	4 tsp.
4 tsp.	lemon juice	2 Tbsp.
½ cup	chopped pecans	1 cup
1½ cups	rolled oats	3 cups
1 cup	all-purpose flour	2 cups
¾ cup	packed brown sugar	1½ cups
½ cup	chopped pecans	1 cup
1 tsp.	baking powder	2 tsp.
½ tsp.	baking soda	1 tsp.
½ tsp.	salt	1 tsp.
⅔ cup	buttermilk	1⅓ cups
2	eggs, lightly beaten	4
¼ cup	butter, melted	½ cup
1½ tsp.	vanilla	3 tsp.
	honey (optional)	

PREP: 40 MINUTES
BAKE: 30 MINUTES
BROIL: 3 MINUTES
COOL: 30 MINUTES
OVEN: 350°F

Oatmeal Cake

Oh, my. This nubby, rustic cake is as warm and comforting as a morning bowl of hearty brown sugar and pecan oatmeal.

8 servings	ingredients	16 servings
1¼ cups	water	2½ cups
¾ cup	rolled oats	1½ cups
¼ cup	butter, cut up	½ cup
1	eggs, lightly beaten	2
¾ cup	packed brown sugar	1½ cups
¾ cup	whole wheat flour	1¼ cups
½ cup	all-purpose flour	1 cup
¾ tsp.	baking soda	1½ tsp.
¾ tsp.	ground cinnamon	1½ tsp.
¼ tsp.	salt	¾ tsp.
¼ tsp.	ground nutmeg	¾ tsp.
¼ cup	butter	½ cup
¾ cup	packed brown sugar	1⅓ cups
¼ cup	half-and-half or light cream	½ cup
1 cup	flaked coconut	2 cups
½ cup	chopped pecans	1 cup
½ tsp.	vanilla	1 tsp.

1. Preheat oven to 350°F. Lightly grease the bottom of a 2-quart baking dish or pan; set pan aside.

2. In a large saucepan bring the water to boiling. Add oats and ¼ cup butter. Reduce heat to low; cook for 5 minutes to soften the oats, stirring occasionally. Remove from heat; set aside.

3. In a large bowl stir together the eggs and the ¾ cup brown sugar; set aside. In a medium bowl stir together the whole wheat flour, all-purpose flour, baking soda, cinnamon, salt, and nutmeg. Using a wooden spoon, stir oat mixture into egg mixture until combined. Fold in flour mixture just until moistened. Spread batter in prepared pan.

4. Bake for 30 to 35 minutes or until a wooden toothpick inserted near the center comes out clean. Remove to a wire rack. Preheat broiler.

5. Meanwhile, in a medium saucepan melt ¼ cup butter. Stir in the ¾ cup brown sugar and the half-and-half until combined. Remove from heat. Stir in coconut, pecans, and vanilla; mix well. Spoon coconut mixture over hot cake.

6. Broil 4 to 5 inches from the heat for 3 to 4 minutes or until topping is bubbly and begins to brown. (Watch closely.) Cool in pan on a wire rack at least 30 minutes before serving. Serve warm or at room temperature.

FOR 16 SERVINGS: Prepare using method above, except in Step 1 use a 3-quart baking dish or pan. In Step 2 use ½ cup butter. In Step 3 use 1½ cups brown sugar. In Step 5 melt ½ cup butter; stir in 1⅓ cups packed brown sugar.

PER SERVING 481 cal., 24 g total fat (13 g sat. fat), 73 mg chol., 378 mg sodium, 64 g carbo., 4 g fiber, 6 g pro.

Busy-Day Cake

As it's name implies, this one-layer cake, which mixes in minutes, is perfect for busy bakers like you.

PREP: **25 MINUTES**
BAKE: **30 MINUTES**   COOL: **30 MINUTES**
OVEN: **350°F**

8 servings	ingredients	16 servings
1⅓ cups	all-purpose flour	2⅔ cups
⅔ cup	sugar	1⅓ cups
2 tsp.	baking powder	4 tsp.
⅔ cup	milk	1⅓ cups
¼ cup	butter, softened	½ cup
1	egg	2
1 tsp.	vanilla	2 tsp.
1 cup	whipping cream	2 cups
2 Tbsp.	sugar	¼ cup
½ tsp.	vanilla	1 tsp.
1½ cups	assorted fresh berries	3 cups

1. Preheat oven to 350°F. Grease an 8×1½-inch round cake pan; set pan aside.

2. In a medium mixing bowl combine flour, sugar, and baking powder. Add milk, butter, egg, and vanilla. Beat with an electric mixer on low until combined. Beat on medium for 1 minute. Spread batter in prepared pan.

3. Bake about 30 minutes or until a wooden toothpick inserted near center comes out clean. Cool cake in pan on a wire rack about 30 minutes.

4. Meanwhile, to prepare sweetened whipped cream, in a chilled mixing bowl add whipping cream, the 2 tablespoons sugar, and the ½ teaspoon vanilla. Beat with an electric mixer on medium until soft peaks form.

5. Serve cake warm with berries and sweetened whipped cream.

FOR 16 SERVINGS: Prepare using method above, except in Step 1 use two 8×1½-inch round cake pans. In Step 2 divide batter evenly between the two pans. In Step 4 use 2 cups whipping cream, ¼ cup sugar, and 1 teaspoon vanilla.

PER SERVING *346 cal., 18 g total fat (11 g sat. fat), 84 mg chol., 130 mg sodium, 42 g carbo., 2 g fiber, 5 g pro.*

Apple Cake with Buttery Caramel Sauce

Add this recipe to your batch of autumn must-make recipes. It is a perfect destination for fall's crop of crisp, juicy apples.

1. Preheat oven to 350°F. Grease a 2-quart rectangular baking dish; set pan aside. In a medium bowl stir together the flour, baking powder, salt, nutmeg, cinnamon, and baking soda; set aside.

2. In a large mixing bowl beat butter with an electric mixer on medium to high for 30 seconds. Gradually add sugar, about ¼ cup at a time, beating on medium until well combined. Scrape sides of bowl; beat for 2 minutes more. Add eggs, one at a time, beating well after each addition. Add flour mixture to butter mixture, beating on low just until combined. Fold in apples and walnuts. (Batter will be thick.) Spread batter in prepared baking pan.

3. Bake for 40 to 45 minutes or until a toothpick inserted near the center comes out clean. Cool in pan on a wire rack for 45 minutes.

4. Meanwhile, for buttery caramel sauce, in a small saucepan melt the 3 tablespoons butter over medium heat. Stir in the 3 tablespoons sugar, brown sugar, and whipping cream. Bring to boiling, stirring constantly. Remove from heat; stir in vanilla.

5. Serve warm cake with warm buttery caramel sauce.

FOR 16 SERVINGS: Prepare using method above, except in Step 1 use a 3-quart rectangular baking dish. Increase baking time to 45 to 50 minutes. In Step 4 melt the ⅓ cup butter; stir in the ⅓ cup sugar, brown sugar, and whipping cream. Continue as directed.

PER SERVING 369 cal., 17 g total fat (8 g sat. fat), 59 mg chol., 188 mg sodium, 23 g carbo., 2 g fiber, 4 g pro.

PREP: 35 MINUTES
BAKE: 40 MINUTES   COOL: 45 MINUTES
OVEN: 350°F

8 servings	ingredients	16 servings
1 cup	all-purpose flour	2 cups
½ tsp.	baking powder	1 tsp.
¼ tsp.	salt	½ tsp.
¼ tsp.	ground nutmeg	½ tsp.
¼ tsp.	ground cinnamon	½ tsp.
⅛ tsp.	baking soda	¼ tsp.
¼ cup	butter, softened	½ cup
1 cup	sugar	2 cups
1	eggs	2
3 cups	coarsely chopped unpeeled cooking apples	6 cups
½ cup	chopped walnuts	1 cup
3 Tbsp.	butter	⅓ cup
3 Tbsp.	sugar	⅓ cup
3 Tbsp.	packed brown sugar	⅓ cup
3 Tbsp.	whipping cream	⅓ cup
¼ tsp.	vanilla	½ tsp.

Mocha Sheetcake with Warm Frosting

Serve this cake to a happy crowd at the next potluck. It's so lusciously rich that a small helping goes a long way.

1. Preheat oven to 350°F. Generously grease a 11×7×2-inch baking pan; set aside.

2. Dissolve 2 teaspoons of the espresso powder in the boiling water. In a medium saucepan combine brewed espresso, ½ cup of the butter, and 3 tablespoons of the unsweetened cocoa. Bring to boiling over medium-high heat, stirring constantly. Remove from heat; let cool for 10 minutes.

3. In a large bowl whisk together the sugar and flour. Add the warm cocoa mixture; stir to blend well. Add eggs, ½ cup of the buttermilk, baking soda, 1 teaspoon of the vanilla, cinnamon, and salt; mix well. Spread batter evenly into prepared pan.

4. Bake for 20 to 25 minutes or until a wooden toothpick inserted near the center comes out clean.

5. Meanwhile, for mocha frosting, in a medium saucepan heat 3 tablespoons of the butter, ¼ cup of the buttermilk, 2 tablespoons of the unsweetened cocoa powder, and ½ teaspoon of the instant espresso coffee powder over medium-low heat until butter melts, stirring constantly. Remove from heat. With an electric mixer on medium, beat in 2¼ cups powdered sugar and 1 teaspoon of the vanilla.

6. Immediately frost hot cake with warm mocha frosting. Sprinkle with pecans. Cool to room temperature before cutting.

FOR 24 SERVINGS: Prepare using method above, except in Step 1 use an 15×10×1-inch baking pan. In Step 2 use 4 teaspoons espresso powder, 1 cup butter, and ⅓ cup unsweetened cocoa powder. In Step 3 use ½ cup of the buttermilk, and 1 teaspoon of the vanilla. For the mocha frosting in Step 5 use ⅓ cup of the butter, ½ cup of the buttermilk, ⅓ cup of the unsweetened cocoa powder, 1 teaspoon of the instant espresso coffee powder, 4½ cups powdered sugar, and 1 teaspoon of the vanilla.

PER SERVING 330 cal., 14 g total fat (7 g sat. fat), 45 mg chol., 192 mg sodium, 50 g carbo., 2 g fiber, 3 g pro.

PREP: **25 MINUTES**
BAKE: **20 MINUTES**
COOL: **1 HOUR**
OVEN: **350°F**

12 servings	ingredients	24 servings
2½ tsp.	instant espresso coffee powder	5 tsp.
½ cup	boiling water	1 cup
⅔ cup	butter	1⅓ cups
⅓ cup	unsweetened cocoa powder	⅔ cup
1 cup	sugar	2 cups
1 cup	all-purpose flour	2 cups
1	eggs, lightly beaten	2
½ cup	buttermilk	1 cup
½ tsp.	baking soda	1 tsp.
1 tsp.	vanilla	2 tsp.
½ tsp.	ground cinnamon	1 tsp.
¼ tsp.	salt	½ tsp.
2¼ cups	powdered sugar	4½ cups
½ cup	chopped, toasted pecans	1 cup

Brownie Pudding Cake

Fudgy, warm, and oh-so-good, this guilty-pleasure dessert is a must on cold winter nights. Enjoy it alone or with a scoop of ice cream.

PREP: 15 MINUTES
BAKE: 40 MINUTES
COOL: 45 MINUTES
OVEN: 350°F

6 servings	ingredients	12 servings
1 cup	all-purpose flour	2 cups
¾ cup	granulated sugar	1½ cups
2 Tbsp.	unsweetened cocoa powder	4 Tbsp.
2 tsp.	baking powder	4 tsp.
¼ tsp.	salt	½ tsp.
½ cup	milk	1 cup
2 Tbsp.	cooking oil	4 Tbsp.
1 tsp.	vanilla	2 tsp.
½ cup	chopped walnuts	1 cup
¾ cup	packed brown sugar	1½ cups
¼ cup	unsweetened cocoa powder	½ cup
1½ cups	boiling water	3 cups
	Sweetened whipped cream (optional)	

1. Preheat oven to 350°F. Grease an 8×8×2-inch baking pan; set aside. In a medium bowl stir together the flour, granulated sugar, the 2 tablespoons cocoa powder, the baking powder, and salt. Stir in the milk, oil, and vanilla. Stir in the walnuts.

2. Pour batter into prepared baking pan. In a small bowl stir together the brown sugar and the ¼ cup cocoa powder. Stir in the boiling water. Slowly pour brown sugar mixture over batter.

3. Bake for 40 minutes. Transfer to a wire rack and cool for 45 to 60 minutes. Serve warm. Spoon cake into dessert bowls; spoon pudding from the bottom of the pan over cake. If desired, serve with sweetened whipped cream.

FOR 12 SERVINGS: Prepare using method above, except in Step 1 use a 3-quart rectangular baking dish and 4 tablespoons cocoa powder. In Step 2 use ½ cup cocoa powder.

PER SERVING 406 cal., 12 g total fat (2 g sat. fat), 2 mg chol., 237 mg sodium, 74 g carbo., 3 g fiber, 5 g pro.

S'Mores Bread Pudding

Camp out in front of the fireplace with a bowl full of this comfort food.

PREP: **25 MINUTES**
STAND: **5 MINUTES**   BAKE: **40 MINUTES**
COOL: **20 MINUTES**   OVEN: **325°F**

9 servings	ingredients	18 servings
4	Hawaiian sweet bread or frankfurter buns, cut into 1-inch pieces	8
4	eggs	8
1 14-oz. can	sweetened condensed milk	2 14-oz. cans
¾ cup	milk	1½ cups
1 tsp.	vanilla	2 tsp.
¼ tsp.	ground nutmeg	½ cup
1 cup	tiny marshmallows	2 cups
¾ cup	semisweet chocolate pieces	1½ cups
½ cup	coarsely crushed graham cracker squares	1 cup
2 Tbsp.	milk	¼ cup

1. Preheat oven to 325°F. Grease a 2-quart square baking dish; set aside. Place bread pieces on shallow baking sheet. Bake for 7 to 8 minutes or until dry and crisp; cool.

2. In a medium bowl lightly beat eggs. Stir in sweetened condensed milk, ¾ cup milk, vanilla, and nutmeg; set aside.

3. Place bread pieces in prepared baking dish. Sprinkle with ½ cup each of the marshmallows and chocolate pieces. Evenly pour milk mixture over all. Let stand 5 minutes. Sprinkle with crushed graham crackers. Bake, uncovered, for 35 minutes. Sprinkle with ¼ cup of the remaining marshmallows. Bake about 5 minutes more or until a knife inserted near center comes out clean.

4. For drizzle, in small saucepan heat and whisk remaining marshmallows, remaining chocolate pieces, and 2 tablespoons milk over low heat until melted and smooth. Drizzle over bread pudding. Cool 20 to 30 minutes before serving. Serve warm.

FOR 18 SERVINGS: Prepare using method above, except in Step 1 use a 3-quart baking dish. In Step 2 use 1½ cups milk. In Step 4 use ¼ cup milk.

PER SERVING *348 cal., 12 g total fat (6 g sat. fat), 111 mg chol., 221 mg sodium, 52 g carbo., 1 g fiber, 10 g pro.*

Deluxe Caramel-Nut Brownies

Anyone who has a hankering for turtle candies will fall in love with these ooey-gooey treats.

1. Preheat oven to 350°F. Line a 2-quart baking pan with heavy foil, extending foil over the edges of the pan. Lightly grease foil; set pan aside.

2. In a large mixing bowl beat butter with an electric mixer on medium to high for 30 seconds. Add brown sugar; beat until fluffy. Add melted chocolate, beating until blended. Beat in eggs and vanilla until combined. Beat in flour. Stir in chocolate pieces and pecans.

3. Evenly spread half the batter in the prepared pan. Bake for 15 minutes. Meanwhile, in a heavy, medium-size saucepan heat and stir caramels and milk over medium-low heat until melted and smooth. Drizzle melted caramels over partially baked brownies. Spread remaining brownie batter evenly over caramel layer.

4. Bake for 25 to 30 minutes more or until edges are set and top appears dry. Cool in pan on a wire rack. Use foil to lift uncut brownies out of pan. Using a hot knife, cut into bars.

FOR 32 SERVINGS: Prepare using method above, except in Step 1 use a 3-quart rectangular baking pan.

PER SERVING *259 cal., 15 g total fat (8 g sat. fat), 42 mg chol., 73 mg sodium, 32 g carbo., 1 g fiber, 3 g pro.*

PREP: 25 MINUTES
BAKE: 40 MINUTES
OVEN: 350°F

16 servings	ingredients	32 servings
½ cup	butter, softened	1 cup
1 cup	packed brown sugar	2 cup
3 oz.	bittersweet baking chocolate, chopped and melted	6 oz.
2	eggs	4
1 tsp.	vanilla	2 tsp.
½ cup	all-purpose flour	1 cup
1 cup	semisweet chocolate pieces	2 cups
½ cup	chopped pecans, toasted	1 cup
12	vanilla caramels, unwrapped	24
1 Tbsp.	milk	2 Tbsp.

Chocolate Bread Pudding

Get an instant chocolate fix with a bowl full of this rich dessert. Top warm pudding with ice cream and let the richness meet its match.

1. Preheat oven to 400°F. Cut bread into ½-inch cubes (you should have about 6 cups). In a large bowl toss bread cubes with melted butter. Transfer buttered bread cubes to a shallow baking pan. Bake for 10 to 12 minutes or until golden brown, stirring once. Set aside.

2. In a medium saucepan combine whipping cream, milk, and 6 ounces of chocolate. Stir over medium heat until chocolate is melted. In a large bowl whisk together egg yolks and sugar. Gradually whisk cream mixture into egg yolks. Stir in toasted bread. Cover and refrigerate 2 hours or overnight.

3. Preheat oven to 325°F. Lightly butter a 2-quart square baking dish. Stir the 4 ounces of chocolate into chilled bread mixture. Pour into prepared dish. Place in a roasting pan. Place pan on rack in oven. Pour boiling water into the roasting pan around baking dish to a depth of 1 inch. Bake, uncovered, about 55 minutes or until evenly puffed and top is set.

4. Carefully remove baking dish from water. Cool about 1 hour on a wire rack. Scoop into serving dishes. Serve with vanilla ice cream.

FOR 16 SERVINGS: Prepare using method above, except in Step 1 you should have about 12 cups of cubed bread. In Step 2 use 12 ounces chocolate. In Step 3 use a 3-quart baking dish and stir in the 8 ounces of chocolate. Increase baking time to 55 to 65 minutes.

PER SERVING 582 cal., 46 g total fat (26 g sat. fat), 268 mg chol., 190 mg sodium, 43 g carbo., 3 g fiber, 8 g pro.

PREP: 35 MINUTES
CHILL: 2 HOURS
BAKE: 1 HOUR 5 MINUTES
COOL: 1 HOUR
OVEN: 400°/325°F

8 servings	ingredients	16 servings
8 oz.	brioche or challah	16 oz.
⅓ cup	unsalted butter, melted	⅔ cup
1½ cups	whipping cream	3 cups
½ cup	milk	1 cup
6 oz.	bittersweet or semisweet chocolate	12 oz.
6	egg yolks	12
⅓ cup	granulated sugar	⅔ cup
4 oz.	bittersweet or semisweet chocolate, coarsely chopped	8 oz.
	Vanilla ice cream	

Macadamia-Eggnog Bars

Buttery-rich macadamias make these bars taste like Christmas in Hawaii. Be sure to refrigerate leftover nuts—these creamy nuts tend to become rancid quickly.

PREP: **25 MINUTES**
BAKE: **25 MINUTES**
OVEN: **350°F**

18 servings	ingredients	36 servings
1 cup	granulated sugar	2 cups
⅓ cup	butter	⅔ cup
1	eggs	2
½ tsp.	vanilla	1¼ tsp.
1 cup	all-purpose flour	2 cups
½ tsp.	baking powder	1 tsp.
¼ tsp.	ground nutmeg	½ tsp.
½ cup	chopped macadamia nuts	1 cup
½ cup	powdered sugar	1 cup
1 tsp.	eggnog	1 Tbsp.

1. Preheat oven to 350°F. Line 2-quart baking pan with foil, grease foil; set aside. In a medium saucepan stir sugar and butter over medium heat until butter is melted. Remove from heat. Cool slightly.

2. Stir eggs and ½ teaspoon of the vanilla into sugar mixture. Stir in flour, baking powder, and nutmeg. Stir in nuts.

3. Spread mixture evenly into prepared pan. Bake for 25 to 30 minutes or until edges just begin to pull way from the sides of the pan. Cool in pan on a wire rack. Use foil to remove bars from pan; place on cutting board. Cut into squares.

4. Meanwhile, for eggnog drizzle, in a small bowl combine powdered sugar, ⅛ teaspoon of the vanilla, and eggnog. Stir in additional eggnog, 1 teaspoon at a time, until icing reaches drizzling consistency. Drizzle icing over bars.

FOR 36 SERVINGS: Prepare using method above, except in Step 1 use a 3-quart rectangular baking pan. In Step 2 use 1 teaspoon vanilla and in Step 4 use ¼ teaspoon vanilla.

PER SERVING *144 cal., 7 g total fat (3 g sat. fat), 21 mg chol., 39 mg sodium, 21 g carbo., 1 g fiber, 1 g pro.*

Oatmeal Jam Bars

This cookie bar doesn't need an introduction. Classic in every sense of the word, this raspberry-lemon bar will be sure to bring back many mom memories.

1. Preheat oven to 350°F. Grease a 9×9×2-inch baking pan; set aside. In a medium bowl stir together flour, baking soda, and salt. Stir in oats, brown sugar, and lemon peel; set aside.

2. In a large mixing bowl combine cream cheese and butter. Beat with an electric mixer on medium to high for 30 seconds. Add flour mixture; beat on low until mixture is crumbly. Measure 1 cup of the crumb mixture; set aside.

3. Press the remaining crumb mixture onto the bottom of the prepared baking pan. Bake for 20 minutes.

4. Meanwhile, in a small bowl combine preserves and lemon juice. Carefully spread preserves mixture over hot crust. Sprinkle with the reserved 1 cup crumb mixture. Bake about 15 minutes more or until top is golden brown. Cool in pan on wire rack. Cut into bars.

FOR 72 SERVINGS: Prepare using method above, except in Step 1 use a 3-quart pan. In Step 2 reserve 2 cups crumb mixture. In Step 4, sprinkle reserved crumb mixture.

PER SERVING 77 cal., 3 g total fat (2 g sat. fat), 9 mg chol., 52 mg sodium, 11 g carbo., 0 g fiber, 1 g pro.

PREP: **15 MINUTES**
BAKE: **35 MINUTES**
OVEN: **350°F**

36 servings	ingredients	72 servings
⅔ cup	all-purpose flour	1⅓ cups
⅛ tsp.	baking soda	¼ tsp.
⅛ tsp.	salt	¼ tsp.
⅓ cup	quick-cooking rolled oats	¾ cup
3 Tbsp.	packed brown sugar	⅓ cup
½ tsp.	finely shredded lemon peel	1 tsp.
1 3-oz. pkg.	cream cheese, softened	2 3-oz. pkgs.
2 Tbsp.	butter, softened	¼ cup
⅓ cup	seedless raspberry preserves	¾ cup
½ tsp.	lemon juice	1 tsp.

Lush Lemon Blondies

A sturdier version of the well-known lemon bar, this chewy blondie is chock-full of chopped macadamia nuts and pockets of lemon curd.

PREP: 30 MINUTES
BAKE: 30 MINUTES
OVEN: 325°F

20 servings	ingredients	40 servings
1½ cups	all-purpose flour	3 cups
1 tsp.	baking powder	2 tsp.
¼ tsp.	salt	½ tsp.
½ cup	butter, softened	1 cup
¾ cup	packed brown sugar	1½ cups
½ cup	granulated sugar	1 cup
2	eggs	4
2 tsp.	vanilla	4 tsp.
½ cup	chopped macadamia nuts, toasted	1 cup
1 10-oz. jar	lemon curd	2 10-oz. jars

1. Preheat oven to 325°F. Line a 9×9×2-inch baking pan with foil, extending the foil over edges of pan. Grease foil; set pan aside.

2. In a medium bowl stir together flour, baking powder, and salt. In a large mixing bowl beat butter with an electric mixer on medium to high for 30 seconds. Add brown sugar and granulated sugar. Beat for 5 minutes, scraping bowl occasionally. Add eggs, one at a time, beating well after each addition. Beat in vanilla. Gradually add flour mixture, beating on low until combined. Stir in ⅓ cup of the macadamia nuts.

3. Spread one-third of the batter in the prepared baking pan. Drop large spoonfuls of lemon curd onto batter at 1-inch intervals. Top with the remaining batter. Gently swirl a knife through the batter and lemon curd layers to marble. Sprinkle with the remaining macadamia nuts.

4. Bake about 30 minutes or until golden and set. Cool in pan on a wire rack. Remove bars from pan, using the foil to lift bars. Place on cutting board; cut into bars.

FOR 40 SERVINGS: Prepare using method above, except in Step 1 use a 3-quart rectangular baking pan. In Step 2 use ¾ cup macadamia nuts.

PER SERVING 204 cal., 8 g total fat (4 g sat. fat), 44 mg chol., 107 mg sodium, 32 g carbo., 2 g fiber, 2 g pro.

Rhubarb Bars

If you're searching for ideas of what to do with this year's harvest of rhubarb other than make rhubarb crisp, bookmark this recipe and add it to your "Can't Wait Until Spring" recipe collection.

1. Preheat oven to 375°F. Line a 2-quart baking pan with foil, extending about 1 inch of foil over the edges of pan. Grease foil; set pan aside.

2. In a medium saucepan stir together the rhubarb, the ½ cup granulated sugar, and the water. Bring to boiling; reduce heat. Cover and simmer for 5 minutes. Meanwhile, in a small bowl stir together ¼ cup granulated sugar and the 1 tablespoon flour. Stir sugar mixture into rhubarb mixture. Cook and stir about 1 minute more or until thick. Remove from heat; stir in vanilla. Set aside.

3. For crust, in a medium bowl stir together the ¾ cup flour, oats, brown sugar, and baking soda. Using a pastry blender, cut in shortening until mixture resembles coarse crumbs. Stir in the ¼ cup nuts. Reserve ½ cup of the crumb mixture for topping.

4. Press the crumb mixture evenly into the bottom of the prepared pan. Spread rhubarb mixture over top. Sprinkle with topping and, if desired, additional chopped nuts. Bake for 30 to 35 minutes or until the top is golden. Cool in pan on a wire rack. Remove bars from pan, using the foil to lift. Place on cutting board; cut into bars.

FOR 45 SERVINGS: Prepare using method above, except in Step 1 use a 3-quart rectangular baking pan. In Step 2 stir together rhubarb and 1 cup sugar. In a small bowl stir together ½ cup sugar and the 2 tablespoons flour. In Step 3 use 1½ cups flour and ½ cup nuts. Reserve 1 cup of the crumb mixture for the topping.

PER SERVING *122 cal., 5 g total fat (1 g sat. fat), 0 mg chol., 10 mg sodium, 17 g carbo., 1 g fiber, 1 g pro.*

PREP: 20 MINUTES
BAKE: 30 MINUTES
COOK: 15 MINUTES
OVEN: 375°F

22 servings	ingredients	45 servings
1½ cups	fresh or frozen unsweetened, sliced rhubarb	3 cups
½ cup	granulated sugar	11 cup
2 Tbsp.	water	¼ cup
¼ cup	granulated sugar	½ cup
1 Tbsp.	all-purpose flour	2 Tbsp.
½ tsp.	vanilla	1 tsp.
¾ cup	all-purpose flour	1½ cups
¾ cups	quick-cooking rolled oats	1½ cups
½ cup	packed brown sugar	1 cup
⅛ tsp.	baking soda	¼ tsp.
½ cup	shortening	1 cup
¼ cup	chopped pecans or walnuts	½ cup
	Chopped pecans or walnuts (optional)	

Almond Brittle Brownies

If you can't resist taking a bite or two of this buttery almond brittle, make sure to save enough for the brownie. The chocolate toffee-almond combination is bound to get rave reviews.

PREP: 30 MINUTES
BAKE: 37 MINUTES
OVEN: 350°F

18 servings	ingredients	36 servings
3 Tbsp.	slivered almonds	⅓ cup
2 Tbsp.	sugar	¼ cup
2 tsp.	butter	1 Tbsp.
¼ cup	butter, softened	½ cup
¼ cup	sugar	½ cup
½ cup	all-purpose flour	1 cup
⅓ cup	butter	¾ cup
2 oz.	unsweetened chocolate, coarsely chopped	4oz.
1 cup	sugar	2 cups
1 tsp.	vanilla	2 tsp.
2	eggs	4
¾ cup	all-purpose flour	1½ cups

1. Preheat oven to 350°F. Line a baking sheet with foil. Butter foil; set baking sheet aside. Grease and flour a 2-quart baking pan; set aside.

2. For almond brittle, in a medium skillet combine almonds, the 2 tablespoons sugar, and the 2 teaspoons butter. Cook over medium-high heat until sugar starts to melt, shaking skillet occasionally. Do not stir. When sugar starts to melt, reduce heat to low and cook until sugar is golden brown, stirring as needed with a wooden spoon. Pour onto the prepared baking sheet; cool.

3. Place almond brittle in a heavy plastic bag. Using a rolling pin or meat mallet, coarsely crush brittle; set aside.

4. For crust, in a medium mixing bowl combine the ¼ cup softened butter and ¼ cup sugar. Beat with an electric mixer on medium to high until smooth. Stir in the ½ cup flour until combined. Press mixture evenly onto the bottom of the prepared baking pan. Bake about 10 minutes or until edges are lightly browned.

5. Meanwhile, in a medium saucepan combine the ⅓ cup butter and chocolate. Stir over low heat until melted. Remove from heat. Stir in 1 cup sugar and vanilla. Add eggs, one at a time, beating with a wooden spoon after each addition just until combined. Stir in the ¾ cup flour. Pour batter over hot crust, spreading evenly.

6. Bake for 15 minutes. Sprinkle with crushed almond brittle; press lightly into chocolate layer. Bake for 12 to 15 minutes more or until top is set. Cool in pan on a wire rack. Cut into bars.

FOR 36 SERVINGS: Prepare using method above, except in Step 1 use a 3-quart rectangular baking pan. In Step 2 use ¼ cup sugar and 1 tablespoon butter. In Step 4 use ½ cup softened butter, ½ cup sugar, and 1 cup flour. In Step 5 use ¾ cup butter, 2 cups sugar, and 1½ cups flour.

PER SERVING 164 cal., 10 g total fat (5 g sat. fat), 41 mg chol., 56 mg sodium, 20 g carbo., 1 g fiber, 2 g pro.

Triple-Chocolate and Espresso Brownies

Get a caffeine and chocolate fix all in one with this brownie. Serve these dark handsome brownies with a piping hot mug of cappuccino or a creamy latte.

1. In a medium saucepan combine butter, bittersweet chocolate, and unsweetened chocolate. Stir over low heat until melted and smooth. Remove from heat; cool. Preheat oven to 350°F. Line an 8×8×2-inch baking pan with heavy foil, extending foil over edges of pan. Grease foil; set pan aside.

2. Stir the sugar into the cooled chocolate mixture. Add the eggs, one at a time, beating with a wooden spoon just until combined. Stir in espresso powder and vanilla. In a small bowl stir together the flour, baking soda, and salt. Add flour mixture to chocolate mixture; stir just until combined. Stir in the 1 cup chocolate pieces. Spread the batter evenly in the prepared pan.

3. Bake for 30 minutes. Cool in pan on a wire rack.

4. For the chocolate cream cheese frosting, in a small saucepan heat and stir the ½ cup semisweet chocolate pieces over low heat until smooth. Remove from heat; let cool. In a medium bowl stir together cream cheese and powdered sugar. Stir in melted chocolate until smooth.

5. Spread the chocolate cream cheese frosting over cooled brownies. Using the edges of the foil, lift uncut brownies from pan. Place on cutting board; cut into squares. If desired, sprinkle with chocolate-covered espresso beans.

FOR 40 SERVINGS: Prepare using method above, except in Step 2 use a 3-quart rectangular baking pan and stir in 2 cups chocolate pieces. In Step 4 in 1 cup semisweet chocolate pieces.

PER SERVING 258 cal., 16 g total fat (9 g sat. fat), 38 mg chol., 85 mg sodium, 30 g carbo., 2 g fiber, 3 g pro.

PREP: 30 MINUTES   BAKE: 30 MINUTES
COOL: 45 MINUTES   OVEN: 350°F

20 servings	ingredients	40 servings
½ cup	butter	1 cup
4 oz.	bittersweet chocolate, coarsely chopped	8 oz.
3 oz.	unsweetened chocolate, coarsely chopped	6 oz.
1 cup	sugar	2 cups
2	eggs	4
1 Tbsp.	espresso powder	2 Tbsp.
1 tsp.	vanilla	2 tsp.
⅔ cup	all-purpose flour	1⅓ cups
¼ tsp.	baking soda	½ tsp.
⅛ tsp.	salt	¼ tsp.
1 cup	miniature semisweet chocolate pieces	2 cups
½ cup	semisweet chocolate pieces	1 cup
1 3-oz. pkg.	cream cheese, softened	2 3-oz. pkgs.
¼ cup	powdered sugar	½ cup
	Chocolate-covered espresso beans, chopped (optional)	

Cherry Crumble Pie Bars

Attention cherry pie lovers, this is just what you've been looking for—an easy-to-make version of the All-American favorite. Cherry pie filling makes them a snap to make.

PREP: **25 MINUTES**
BAKE: **55 MINUTES**
OVEN: **350°F**

16 servings	ingredients	32 servings
1 cups	all-purpose flour	2 cups
⅔ cups	finely ground almonds	1¼ cups
⅓ cup	packed brown sugar	¾ cup
½ cup	butter, cut up	1 cup
⅓ cup	granulated sugar	¾ cup
2 tsp.	cornstarch	1 Tbsp.
¼ tsp.	finely shredded lemon peel	½ tsp.
2 cups	frozen unsweetened pitted tart red cherries, thawed and drained	4 cups
¼ tsp.	almond extract	½ tsp.

1. Preheat oven to 350°F. Line a 2-quart rectangular baking pan with foil, extending foil over the edges of the pan; set aside.

2. For crust, in a large bowl stir together the flour, almonds, and brown sugar. Using a pastry blender, cut in the butter until mixture resembles fine crumbs. Remove ¾ cup of the crust mixture; set aside. Press the remaining mixture evenly onto the bottom of prepared baking pan. Bake for 15 minutes.

3. Meanwhile, for filling, in another large bowl combine the granulated sugar, cornstarch, and lemon peel. Add cherries and almond extract; toss gently to combine. Spoon cherry filling over hot baked crust, spreading evenly (mixture will be wet). Sprinkle with reserved crust mixture.

4. Bake about 40 minutes or until filling is bubbly and topping is lightly browned. Cool in pan on a wire rack. Using the edges of the foil, lift cherry crumble out of the pan. Invert onto a baking sheet; remove foil. Invert again onto a cutting board. Cut into bars.

FOR 32 SERVINGS: Prepare using method above, except in Step 1 use a 3-quart rectangular baking pan. In Step 2 remove 1½ cups of the crust mixture.

PER SERVING 148 cal., 7 g total fat (4 g sat. fat), 15 mg chol., 43 mg sodium, 19 g carbo., 1 g fiber, 2 g pro.

Five-Layer Bars

Although there are several versions of this five-layer coconut bar, this one may be the absolute best. You'll love the combination of crushed coconut macaroons and chocolate—plus the addition of dried cranberries and nuts make them a perfect holiday bar.

1. Preheat oven to 350°F. Arrange cookies in a greased 2-quart baking dish or pan. Press cookies together to form a crust.

2. Bake for 12 minutes. Sprinkle crust with chocolate pieces, dried cranberries, and peanuts. Drizzle with condensed milk.

3. Bake for 25 minutes or until edges are light brown. Cool in pan on a wire rack. Cut into bars.

FOR 30 SERVINGS: Prepare using method above, except in Step 1 use a 3-quart baking dish or pan.

PER SERVING *181 cal., 7 g total fat (4 g sat. fat), 3 mg chol., 86 mg sodium, 28 g carbo., 1 g fiber, 3 g pro.*

PREP: **10 MINUTES**
BAKE: **37 MINUTES**   OVEN: **350°F**

15 servings	ingredients	30 servings
1 10-oz. pkg.	soft coconut macaroon cookies	2 10-oz. pkgs.
6 Tbsp.	semisweet chocolate pieces	¾ cup
6 Tbsp.	dried cranberries or raisins	¾ cup
½ cup	coarsely chopped peanuts	1 cup
½ cup	sweetened condensed milk	1 cup

Peach Turnovers

Frozen puff pastry has a way of making even beginning bakers look like rock stars. Once you see how easy they are to use you'll be filling them with all sorts of other fruits.

PREP: 25 MINUTES
BAKE: 15 MINUTES
OVEN: 400°F

4 servings	ingredients	8 servings
2 Tbsp.	granulated sugar	¼ cup
1 Tbsp.	all-purpose flour	2 Tbsp.
⅛ tsp.	ground cinnamon	¼ tsp.
1⅓ cups	chopped peach, nectarine, or chopped peeled apple	2⅔ cups
½ of a 17.3-oz. pkg.	frozen puff pastry sheets, thawed	1 17.3-oz. pkg.
	Milk	
	Coarse sugar (optional)	
¾ cup	powdered sugar	1½ cups
1 Tbsp.	butter, softened	2 Tbsp.
½ tsp.	vanilla	1 tsp.
Dash	salt	⅛ tsp.
2 tsp.	milk	4 tsp.

1. Preheat oven to 400°F. Line a large baking sheet with parchment paper; set aside. For filling, in a small bowl stir together granulated sugar, flour, and cinnamon. Add chopped peaches; toss to coat.

2. Unfold pastry. Cut pastry into 4 squares. Brush edges of squares with milk. Evenly spoon filling onto centers of squares. Fold one corner of a square over filling to opposite corner. Press edges with the tines of a fork to seal. Place turnover on prepared baking sheet. Prick tops of turnovers several times with a fork. Brush with additional milk and, if desired, sprinkle with coarse sugar.

3. Bake for 15 to 18 minutes or until puffed and golden brown. Cool slightly on baking sheet on a wire rack.

4. Meanwhile, in a small bowl stir together the powdered sugar, butter, vanilla, and salt. Add enough milk to make icing of drizzling consistency. Drizzle over warm turnovers.

FOR 8 SERVINGS: Prepare using method above, except in Step 2 cut pastry in 8 squares.

PER SERVING *507 cal., 27 g total fat (8 g sat. fat), 8 mg chol., 213 mg sodium, 63 g carbo., 2 g fiber, 5 g pro.*

Strawberry-Raspberry-Rhubarb Crumble

The harbingers of spring appear when you crave them the most. Try to find strawberries that do not have green or white "shoulders"—they'll be sweeter and more juicy.

PREP: 30 MINUTES
BAKE: 1 HOUR 25 MINUTES
OVEN: 375°F

6 servings	ingredients	12 servings
¾ cup	all-purpose flour	1⅔ cups
¼ cup	packed brown sugar	½ cup
½ cup	slivered almonds (optional)	1 cup
1 tsp.	baking powder	2 tsp.
1 tsp.	finely shredded lemon peel	2 tsp.
¼ cup	butter, melted	½ cup
3 cups	fresh strawberries, hulled and quartered	6 cups
1½ cups	fresh rhubarb, cut into ½-inch slices	3 cups
1 cup	fresh raspberries	2 cups
½ cup	granulated sugar	1 cup
¼ tsp.	cornstarch	½ tsp.
⅛ tsp.	salt	¼ tsp.
1 Tbsp.	Chambord or raspberry liqueur (optional)	2 Tbsp.
	Vanilla ice cream (optional)	

1. Preheat oven to 375°F. Butter a 2-quart rectangular baking dish; set aside.

2. For topping, in a medium bowl stir together the flour, brown sugar, almonds (if desired), baking powder, and lemon peel. Add melted butter; mix until clumps form. Cover and chill topping while preparing filling.

3. For filling, in a very large bowl combine strawberries, rhubarb, raspberries, the granulated sugar, the cornstarch, and salt; toss well to combine. If desired, drizzle Chambord over fruit mixture; toss gently to combine. Transfer filling to prepared baking dish. (If using frozen fruit, allow fruit mixture to stand for 45 minutes at room temperature.)

4. Remove topping from the refrigerator. Cover filling evenly with the topping. Place baking dish in a 15×10×1-inch baking pan.

5. Bake about 1 hour and 25 minutes or until fruit is bubbly in the center and topping is golden. If necessary, cover with foil the last 30 minutes of baking to prevent topping from overbrowning. Serve warm or at room temperature. If desired, serve with ice cream.

FOR 12 SERVINGS: Prepare using method above, except in Step 1 use a 3-quart baking dish.

PER SERVING 287 cal., 8 g total fat (5 g sat. fat), 20 mg chol., 166 mg sodium, 53 g carbo., 4 g fiber, 3 g pro.

Apple Crisp

Hot caramel apple slices topped with a crunchy oat streusel and a pool of melting ice cream spell C-O-M-F-O-R-T on a plate.

1. Preheat oven to 375°F. In a large bowl combine apples and granulated sugar. Transfer to a 1½- to 2-quart square baking dish; set aside.

2. For topping, in a medium bowl combine the oats, brown sugar, flour, and cinnamon. Cut in butter until mixture resembles coarse crumbs. Stir in the nuts. Sprinkle topping over apple mixture.

3. Bake for 35 to 40 minutes or until apples are tender and topping is golden. If desired, serve warm with ice cream.

FOR 12 SERVINGS: Prepare using method above, except in Step 1 use a 3-quart baking dish.

PER SERVING *298 cal., 12 g total fat (5 g sat. fat), 20 mg chol., 60 mg sodium, 49 g carbo., 3 g fiber, 3 g pro.*

PREP: **25 MINUTES**
BAKE: **35 MINUTES**
OVEN: **375°F**

6 servings	ingredients	12 servings
6 cups	sliced, peeled cooking apples	12 cups
3 Tbsp.	granulated sugar	6 Tbsp.
½ cup	regular rolled oats	1 cup
½ cup	packed brown sugar	1 cup
¼ cup	all-purpose flour	½ cup
¼ tsp.	ground cinnamon, ginger, or nutmeg	½ tsp.
¼ cup	butter	½ cup
¼ cup	chopped nuts or flaked coconut	½ cup
	Vanilla ice cream (optional)	

Index

Metric Information

PRODUCT DIFFERENCES

Most of the ingredients called for in the recipes in this book are available in most countries. However, some are known by different names. Here are some common American ingredients and their possible counterparts:

- Sugar (white) is granulated, fine granulated, or castor sugar.
- Powdered sugar is icing sugar.
- All-purpose flour is enriched, bleached or unbleached white household flour. When self-rising flour is used in place of all-purpose flour in a recipe that calls for leavening, omit the leavening agent (baking soda or baking powder) and salt.
- Light-color corn syrup is golden syrup.
- Cornstarch is cornflour.
- Baking soda is bicarbonate of soda.
- Vanilla or vanilla extract is vanilla essence.
- Green, red, or yellow sweet peppers are capsicums or bell peppers.
- Golden raisins are sultanas.

VOLUME AND WEIGHT

The United States traditionally uses cup measures for liquid and solid ingredients. The chart (above right) shows the approximate imperial and metric equivalents. If you are accustomed to weighing solid ingredients, the following approximate equivalents will be helpful.

- 1 cup butter, castor sugar, or rice = 8 ounces = ½ pound = 250 grams
- 1 cup flour = 4 ounces = ¼ pound = 125 grams
- 1 cup icing sugar = 5 ounces = 150 grams
- Canadian and U.S. volume for a cup measure is 8 fluid ounces (237 ml), but the standard metric equivalent is 250 ml.
- 1 British imperial cup is 10 fluid ounces.
- In Australia, 1 tablespoon equals 20 ml, and there are 4 teaspoons in the Australian tablespoon.
- Spoon measures are used for smaller amounts of ingredients. Although the size of the tablespoon varies slightly in different countries, for practical purposes and for recipes in this book, a straight substitution is all that's necessary. Measurements made using cups or spoons always should be level unless stated otherwise.

COMMON WEIGHT RANGE REPLACEMENTS

Imperial / U.S.	Metric
½ ounce	15 g
1 ounce	25 g or 30 g
4 ounces (¼ pound)	115 g or 125 g
8 ounces (½ pound)	225 g or 250 g
16 ounces (1 pound)	450 g or 500 g
1¼ pounds	625 g
1½ pounds	750 g
2 pounds or 2¼ pounds	1,000 g or 1 Kg

OVEN TEMPERATURE EQUIVALENTS

Fahrenheit Setting	Celsius Setting	Gas Setting
300°F	150°C	Gas Mark 2 (very low)
325°F	160°C	Gas Mark 3 (low)
350°F	180°C	Gas Mark 4 (moderate)
375°F	190°C	Gas Mark 5 (moderate)
400°F	200°C	Gas Mark 6 (hot)
425°F	220°C	Gas Mark 7 (hot)
450°F	230°C	Gas Mark 8 (very hot)
475°F	240°C	Gas Mark 9 (very hot)
500°F	260°C	Gas Mark 10 (extremely hot)
Broil	Broil	Grill

*Electric and gas ovens may be calibrated using celsius. However, for an electric oven, increase celsius setting 10 to 20 degrees when cooking above 160°C. For convection or forced air ovens (gas or electric), lower the temperature setting 25°F/10°C when cooking at all heat levels.

BAKING PAN SIZES

Imperial / U.S.	Metric
9×1½-inch round cake pan	22- or 23×4-cm (1.5 L)
9×1½-inch pie plate	22- or 23×4-cm (1 L)
8×8×2-inch square cake pan	20×5-cm (2 L)
9×9×2-inch square cake pan	22- or 23×4.5-cm (2.5 L)
11×7×1½-inch baking pan	28×17×4-cm (2 L)
2-quart rectangular baking pan	30×19×4.5-cm (3 L)
13×9×2-inch baking pan	34×22×4.5-cm (3.5 L)
15×10×1-inch jelly roll pan	40×25×2-cm
9×5×3-inch loaf pan	23×13×8-cm (2 L)
2-quart casserole	2 L

U.S./STANDARD METRIC EQUIVALENTS

⅛ teaspoon = 0.5 ml	
¼ teaspoon = 1 ml	
½ teaspoon = 2 ml	
1 teaspoon = 5 ml	
1 tablespoon = 15 ml	
2 tablespoons = 25 ml	
¼ cup = 2 fluid ounces = 50 ml	
⅓ cup = 3 fluid ounces = 75 ml	
½ cup = 4 fluid ounces = 125 ml	
⅔ cup = 5 fluid ounces = 150 ml	
¾ cup = 6 fluid ounces = 175 ml	
1 cup = 8 fluid ounces = 250 ml	
2 cups = 1 pint = 500 ml	
1 quart = 1 litre	